Studies in the Humanities
Literature—Politics—Society

Guy Mermier
General Editor

Vol. 48

PETER LANG
New York • Washington, D.C./Baltimore • Boston
Bern • Frankfurt am Main • Berlin • Vienna • Paris

Justine Rydzeski

Radical Nostalgia in the Age of *Piers Plowman*

Economics, Apocalypticism, and Discontent

PETER LANG
New York • Washington, D.C./Baltimore • Boston
Bern • Frankfurt am Main • Berlin • Vienna • Paris

Library of Congress Cataloging-in-Publication Data

Rydzeski, Justine.
Radical nostalgia in the age of Piers Plowman: economics, apocalypticism, and discontent / Justine Rydzeski.
p. cm. — (Studies in the humanities; vol. 48)
Includes bibliographical references and index.
1. Langland, William, 1330?–1400? Piers the Plowman. 2. Apocalyptic literature—History and criticism. 3. Economics and literature—England—History—To 1500. 4. England—Economic conditions—1066–1485. 5. Radicalism—England—History—To 1500. 6. Tyler's Insurrection, 1381. 7. Radicalism in literature. 8. Discontent in literature. 9. Nostalgia in literature. I. Title
II. Series: Studies in the humanities (New York, N.Y.); vol. 48.
PR2017.A65R84 821′.1—dc21 98-30631
ISBN 0-8204-4273-9
ISSN 0742-6712

Die Deutsche Bibliothek-CIP-Einheitsaufnahme

Rydzeski, Justine:
Radical nostalgia in the age of Piers Plowman: economics, apocalypticism, and discontent / Justine Rydzeski.
–New York; Washington, D.C./Baltimore; Boston; Bern; Frankfurt am Main; Berlin; Vienna; Paris: Lang.
(Studies in the humanities; Vol. 48)
ISBN 0-8204-4273-9

The paper in this book meets the guidelines for permanence and durability of the Committee on Production Guidelines for Book Longevity of the Council of Library Resources.

Printed in the United States of America

For Mary Witt Fleming Heitzig and Mary Varrichio Rydzeski

Acknowledgments

I would like to thank Dr. Michael Kuczynski for his careful reading and his invaluable guidance and Dr. Roy Liuzza and Dr. Gary Remer for their encouragement and confidence in my work. I am also thankful to Dale McDaniel and Hallie Stein Gorup for sharing my work space over the years. I am thankful to Allys Dierker for her continued encouragement. I am also grateful to Dr. Steve Siegel for his support and for helping me stay on schedule and to the late Louise Graham for our conversations on the Antichrist. I would like to acknowledge the financial support I received for this research at Tulane University from the Paul and Elizabeth Selley Doctoral Dissertation Fund as well as the help I had preparing this manuscript for publication from Benjamin Hallman at Peter Lang Publishing. Most of all, I would like to thank Dr. Frank Dodaro for his patience, support, and computer expertise during this project and over the past twenty years.

TABLE OF CONTENTS

Introduction 1

1. *Piers Plowman* and the History of Apocalypticism 11

2. Economics and Salvation: Paying for Sin and Reaping Reward 29

3. Demographics and Discontent in Fourteenth-Century England 55

4. Fellowship and Apocalypticism: *Piers Plowman* and the Nature of Association 71

5. Reading and Rebellion: Imagining Radical Change and the 1381 Revolt 95

Conclusion 115

Notes 129

Bibliography 161

Index 169

INTRODUCTION

Piers Plowman and the Turbulent Fourteenth Century

When Meed makes her entrance in the fourteenth-century poem *Piers Plowman*, she appears as both generous lady and glittering whore. Among her jewels and finery, she seems to bear the weight of centuries of venality satire. Yet according to John A. Yunck, while attacks on wealth, especially those directed at lawyers and the clergy, are fairly common in medieval Latin and French, virtually no venality satire appears in English before 1350;[1] in the second half of the fourteenth century, however, the theme of venality "appears almost everywhere."[2] Lady Meed makes her entrance at a critical time in the development of England's economy, at that moment when the feudal and religious affiliations that bound society together faced the challenges of proto-capitalism. Lady Meed embodies the contradictions of England's economy, a feudal gift economy corrupted by maintenance, bribery, and avarice.

While the economic pressures on England after the 1349 plague intensified complaints about misuses of money and power, the tensions between money and morality in *Piers Plowman* reflect a more deeply rooted moral opposition between the holy poor and the damned rich, a tension destined to increase with the development of England's economy. As Lester Little explains, "[a]daptation to the profit economy . . . . created tensions between morality and behaviour, between theology and society, between religion and life itself."[3] Despite Meed's defense that she offers right reward and payment for work done, she clearly opposes Holy Church and the peaceful rule of the realm. The Meed episode, according to Yunck,

> establish[es] for Langland the fundamental importance of uncontrolled *munera* as a social evil, the chief of all the evils which afflict the Field Full of Folk as organized

> society. The lady in white, Holy Church, is the guide of the Folk to their supernatural end as men; but lady Meed is her eternal opponent, the gracious and attractive epiphany of venal worldliness, who distracts society from that end.[4]

In her acts, Meed is anti-Christ: she could work for Holy Church, but she usually works against her. As we see from her potential marriage partners, Meed is far more likely to marry False than Conscience. Meed, a whore, will sell even herself, and her opposition to Holy Church helps us identify Meed as part of the company of Antichrist, a figure reminiscent of the whore of Babylon from Revelations; Langland thus reinforces the opposition he posits at the beginning of his poem between the dungeon and the tower[5] and helps establish the poem's apocalyptic framework.

The moral peril of money pervades Christian literature, and the concept of redemption itself is fundamentally economic. For Langland, economic metaphors dominate discussions of penance, salvation, and administration of justice. First through the sacrament of penance and later on Judgment Day, exchanges that are economic in nature determine an individual's place in heaven or hell, where one reaps just rewards or receives just punishments, depending upon which type of treasure, earthly or heavenly, one has stored up here. Not only individual, but communal salvation is at stake in *Piers Plowman*; the idealized agricultural world Langland envisions waits on individual reform.

As an apocalypse, *Piers Plowman* reveals Langland's anxiety over the unstable values of his society and his language as the medieval economy based in religious and "natural" or intrinsic value gave way to one based in secular politics and monetary value. This study examines the economic exchanges implicit in the Christian concepts of redemption and satisfaction; discusses the role of famine, plague, and the changing economy in sharpening apocalyptic expectations in fourteenth-century England; explores Langland's handling of the Christian model of history, the apocalyptic model, as a means to express moral and economic crisis and to proclaim impending change and renewal; and investigates how the rebels of 1381 modified apocalyptic commonplaces and the language and scheme of *Piers Plowman* to suit their particular political purposes and to gain popular support.

Apocalyptic writers from the Old Testament onward announce a gap between the expectations and experiences of religious peoples, and they express their anxiety and hope for the future through forecasts of doom and visions of messianic kingdoms. As registers of contemporary injustices and hopes, medieval apocalyptic writings record the dissonance between medieval ethics and experience. Once religious persecution was no longer the threat it was for early Christians, moralists turned their railing against economic persecutors both real and imagined, from tax collectors to bogeymen usurers.

When confronting deteriorating economic and social conditions, Christians often turn to religious explanations and hopes, which can often give rise to apocalyptic exhortations of impending change.[6] In Christian society, the nationalistic and xenophobic attitudes that economic contractions usually foster typically lead to messianic hopes. In his study of revolutionary messianism, Norman Cohn points out that millenarianism tends to reoccur in "the minds of the unprivileged, the oppressed, the disoriented and the unbalanced."[7] A "salvationist movement" is most likely to erupt whenever sudden or significant changes in economic life leave "journeymen and unskilled workers, peasants without land or with too little land to support them, beggars and vagabonds, the unemployed and those threatened with unemployment, the many who for one reason or another could find no assured and recognised place."[8] Such segments of the population "formed the most impulsive and unstable elements in medieval society,"[9] particularly when "their own traditional way of life was becoming impossible."[10] In the waning days of feudalism, as demographic shifts and the developing market economy challenged the traditional means of production and the established social organization, both of which were based in agriculture, feudal organization was indeed becoming "impossible."

One indication of the strain on feudal organization is the increasing frequency of peasant revolts in the later Middle Ages. Rodney Hilton points out the relationship between economic development and social discontent, noting that from the eleventh century on, the "tension between the developing market economy of the peasants and the system of social relations between themselves and those who not only owned land but jurisdictions" resulted in "peasant movements all over Europe."[11] Hilton stresses the relationship between economic growth and discontent, noting that "it was normally in the most developed regions economically that discontent reached the point where fundamental social change seemed the only way out."[12]

As the country's most economically developed region, southeast England bore the brunt of rebel action in 1381. As Hilton reports, "the most industrialized and commercialized part of the country," the southeast, "was the area where lord-peasant relationships (or if one likes to use the expression, the feudal relationships which had been born of a natural economy) were pushed to the limit."[13] The economic development of the southeast, marked by "the coexistence of contrasting social structures, the persistence of the archaic side by side with the foreshadowings of modern social forms,"[14] upset the limited market economy England had enjoyed, and local economies began to provide more and more materials for the expanding international markets, particularly for the wool market.

Another sign of the tension between feudal organization and the growing economy is the nature of rebel demands. Paradoxically, the rebel insistence on customary treatment often accompanied calls for social change when custom worked in the complainants' favor by limiting or granting taxation, through establishing rents, fair prices and wages, or by regulating the movement and availability of labor. On the one hand, the rebels of the English Uprising of 1381 destroyed manorial records that registered their customary duties to local lords; on the other hand, they insisted on their own customarily limited taxation and ancient land rights. Selectively asserting ancient rights, the rebels chose evidence from an idealized feudal past in an opportunistic attempt to legitimize their demands. The rebels thus used unorthodox means to assert an orthodox vision. Likewise, when medieval visionaries like Langland tried to imagine a way out of social crises, they often reverted to the very system they sought to change. For conservative radicals, solutions lay not in changing the economic or social system, but in administering it properly.

Reverting to the past to imagine the future did not, of course, provide new or flexible models to explain why the tripartite estates system was not working. Hopes of reform were bound for frustration, for as Rodney Hilton explains, the traditional medieval theory about the social order "was unrealistic because it did not allow for social mobility and was uneasy about accepting new social groups which emerged owing to the increasing complexity of the economy."[15] At a time when journeymen climbed socially and economically and when churchmen wielded considerable economic and political power, radical visionaries like Langland asserted traditional values and social divisions. While we can surmise like Hilton, with our twentieth-century hindsight, that "conflict over the distribution of the social product was inevitably built into the landlord-tenant system," the traditional view of Langland and his contemporaries affirms instead that social conflicts arose "only because of sinful departure, usually (though not invariably) by the ruled, from obedience in their allotted tasks."[16] For Christian thinkers, each act of disobedience in the present replays the original act of disobedience of Adam and Eve, the source of sin and disobedience in the fallen world, and this traditional medieval approach to social problems—that conflicts are the result of sinful deviation from the traditional tripartite organization of medieval society in which the religious prayed, the lords fought, and the workers worked—left poets like Langland and Gower pondering the future of their declining world.

The nostalgia for a golden past ranges from laments on current times to Edenic fantasies. Cohn notes that when these nostalgic yearnings are projected into the future, they often find expression in millenarian representations:

> the mission which most attracted these masses from the neediest strata of the population was—naturally enough—a mission which was intended to culminate in a total transformation of society. In the eschatological phantasies which they had inherited form the distant past, the forgotten world of early Christianity, these people found a social myth most perfectly adapted to their needs.[17]

Christian ideals of poverty and community and the primitive model of the early Church are especially attractive for the economically oppressed, as is the chiliastic promise of an ever-present savior who sees all and will eventually mete out justice. The phrase "radical nostalgia" in this study addresses this backwards glance that disguises itself as a vision of the future, this longing for early Christian roots as the basis for social regeneration.

Chapter 1, "*Piers Plowman* and the History of Apocalypticism," examines the importance of apocalyptic thinking to medieval notions of history. Biblical authority supports two different visions of history and salvation: one is regenerative and rural and promises a restored earthly paradise; the other is teleological, eschatological, and urban, culminating in the vision of the New Jerusalem. While the early Church accommodated both views, its development into a powerful institution concerned with regulating moral behavior, and the influence of thinkers like Augustine, hastened the growth of the urban vision into an interiorized eschatology, a vision of salvation in which each person endures a microcosm of the Final Judgment in the form of individual judgment soon after the moment of death.

Balanced between the two traditions is the concept of the Millennium—sometimes expected as an era of peace on earth, whether Edenic or as a holy city, and sometimes entirely discredited. In the later Middle Ages, the Church nurtured the urban, eschatological vision, while the tradition that promised the great *renovatio mundi* fell mostly to literary, popular, and sometimes heretical culture. Langland's vision of a restored world and his idealized plowman clearly place him in the agricultural, regenerative tradition, while the movement of the individual from "dowel" to "dobet" to "dobest" represents the individual's salvation and the linear, eschatological view of history. At the end of the B-text, Holy Church is a barn infiltrated by Antichrist, an agricultural society in crisis, poised for justice and renewal.

Chapter 2, "Economics and Salvation: Paying for Sin and Reaping Reward," discusses the conflated nature of economic and religious ideas in the Middle Ages and explores the relationship between individual and communal salvation, examining concepts such as redemption and satisfaction as salvific exchanges. While Jewish and early Christian notions of redemption reflect their origins in the sacrifices of the Old Testament, by the fourteenth century the physical sacrifice of the blood price had given way to a doctrine of satisfaction expressed in metaphors of monetary exchange. The preponderance of agricultural images and metaphors in apocalyptic representations promises regeneration of both the physical world and society and inspires conceptions of the Millennium. The agricultural signs and metaphors in apocalyptic representations often suggest the proper "work" for salvation, a problem with which Langland is preoccupied throughout *Piers Plowman*. Chapter 2 also discusses how changes in the administration of the sacrament of penance put additional emphasis on the sinners' intentions and reflected the growing importance of working for salvation and of labor in general.

The Church's idealization of poverty like Christ's and its insistence that the rich were responsible for the relief of the poor provided a basis for ethical economic and political life which was reinforced by the threat of damnation. Harry A. Miskimin describes the role the church played in establishing and maintaining ethical and political guidelines, noting that the Church "constituted a significant force in the organization, structure, and contemporary conceptions of economic activity and fiscal policy,"[18] and that "[p]rivate property, the inherent value of the individual, and the constraint upon the state to act for the public welfare are economic as well as ethical concepts."[19]

In the turbulent fourteenth century, however, the clash between the values of the Church and its actions as an economic and political entity became painfully evident, particularly to members of the lower clergy. Rodney Hilton points out the unusually conspicuous role that the clergy played in the English revolts:

> There is nothing new in the idea that social rebels of any class should seize on those elements in the literary and homiletic tradition which would legitimize their actions. What needs explaining is the comparatively prominent part played by the lower clergy in south-eastern England, an explanation which cannot be satisfactorily based simply on economic grievances, important though these were.[20]

This study suggests that the lower clergy became involved with the English rebels not just because of possible class associations, but because the religious tradition on which biblical justice is based is infused with economic metaphors, especially agricultural ones—and the agricultural sector was the very sector of the economy that suffered the most in the fourteenth century. I do not mean to imply here that clerics who participated in the rebellion or its planning self-consciously linked their work as laborers in God's vineyard or shepherds of God's flock with a need to reform the real agricultural system and thus to become rebel leaders, but that the Bible's agricultural metaphors provided a framework that made clerics think of their work in terms of agricultural labor, so that upheaval in that sector of the economy was bound to affect the directions in which pastors felt called to lead their flocks. Fusing biblical metaphors and contemporary circumstance, finding the harvest of the apocalypse a ready model for a revolt rural in character, the 1381 rebels imagined their violent actions within the traditional historical framework of Christianity.

Chapter 3 of this study, "Economics and Discontent in Fourteenth-Century England," examines demographic shifts, changes in the money supply, and imbalances of trade in order to present an overview of the economic trends that stimulated discontent in the late fourteenth century. Economists and historians of fourteenth-century England are lucky to have an array of data available for analysis, including mint figures, taxation records, and wills and petitions, but analysis of this data has not yielded a consensus on the economic activity of the period. Miskimin points out conflicting observations by two groups of historians: one group finds the period prosperous when regarding rising wool exports; the other, including M. M. Postan, finds a recession or depression by regarding "falling levels of domestic capital and industry."[21] These conflicting observations signal a rift in England's economic and social organization and suggest that impressions of prosperity or depression depend on just which sector of the economy one examines: in general, the fourteenth century saw the rich get richer and the poor get poorer, and the frustration of those becoming poorer became fuel for the era's apocalyptic hopes.

Any study of the relationship between economics and apocalypticism in the fourteenth and early fifteenth centuries is further complicated by the status of economics in the Middle Ages. According to the *Oxford English Dictionary*, the concept of economics as a means of household management is unfamiliar in England until the sixteenth century, and the idea of economic management of a nation's affairs is unfamiliar until the eighteenth century. Economic discourse in the Middle Ages therefore was inseparable from the religious discourse that managed economic life. As K. Polanyi and C. Arensberg explain, "the facts of the economy were originally embedded in situations that were not in themselves of an economic nature, neither the ends nor the means being primarily material."[22] The "maze of relationships in which the economy is embedded"[23] in the later Middle Ages becomes increasingly difficult to navigate as agricultural crises, plague, and the concentration of wealth leave what was left of feudal life in England in shambles. The shift from a social organization based on subsistence farming, loyalty to local lords, and protection of land and labor to a more mobile society that sought to produce excess, to increase profits, and to manage wages did not often find expression in economic terms, save in the form of specific complaints of affliction from those hardest hit by such changes. More often, medieval Christians express claims of economic affliction through religious language and conventions, and of all the forms and conventions available to fourteenth-century Christians, apocalyptic writing provided the most effective means to explore current injustices and to proclaim impending change.

Chapter 4, "Fellowship and Apocalypticism: *Piers Plowman* and the Nature of Association," explores the changing basis of fellowship and society in the fourteenth century and examines the clash between the beginnings of the capitalist economy and the values of feudal and religious life. Adapting the apocalyptic scheme of the saved and the damned in final conflict, Langland presents a society divided into fellowships of good and evil, of Holy Church and Meed. The millennial society awaited in *Piers Plowman* is marked by its conservative roots; while radical in the sense that he wished society to return to early Christian roots, Langland envisioned a transformed society by reinscribing traditional social organization and orthodox religious belief.

For Langland, the surest way to determine whether one is in the company of good fellows or bad, of Piers or Lady Meed, is by observing one's works and one's companions. The corruption of Lady Meed's retinue is indicated by her followers' ontological degeneration, their reduction to actual or metaphorical animals. This familiar topos is employed not only by Langland to indicate immoderate and inappropriate desire, but by the chroniclers of the 1381 revolt, who describe the rebels as animals to underscore their irrational violence and to suggest that, within the apocalyptic framework, the rebels are fellows of the devil acting against the true Church.

Chapter 5, "Reading and Rebellion: Imagining Change and the 1381 Revolt," explores the rebels' manipulation of Langland's language and imagery. In the hands of revolutionaries, Langland's apocalyptic imagery, potentially inflammatory language, and calls for reform are no longer the musings of conservative idealists, but the fuel for social action. When John Ball and other rebel leaders reiterate the spiritual allegory of Piers Plowman—the progression from *dowel* to *dobet* to *dobest*—so that Langland's salvific pilgrimage becomes a series of codewords, or "watchwords of insurgency" in the words of W. W. Skeat,[24] to indicate stages of the revolt, they transform the allegorical framework of *Piers Plowman* into a plan and rationale for action.

This study concludes by examining the legacy of *Piers Plowman* and surveying the significance of plowman figures in poetic works which *Piers Plowman* inspired. Poems such as *Mum and the Sothsegger*, *Pierce the Ploughman's Crede* and *The Complaint of the Ploughman* demonstrate how poets advocating religious and social reform adapted the language and imagery of *Piers Plowman* to further their own causes. Such poems often reflect the changing economic realities of the later Middle Ages and eventually embrace idealized work as the means for attaining the kingdom on earth and for earning individual salvation. Exploring the relationship between the growth of capitalism and the beginnings of the Reformation, I conclude this study by describing changing late-medieval attitudes towards the Church, its proper work, and the works its believers should perform in order to earn salvation and renew society.

CHAPTER ONE

Piers Plowman and the History of Apocalypticism

Like the history of apocalyptic belief, *Piers Plowman* offers a sometimes oppositional, sometimes complementary pairing of two visions of history. The eschatological vision promises linear progress, the movement of holy individuals and of society at the time of the resurrection of the dead toward the heavenly city. The regenerative vision, the hope of a great *renovatio mundi* in this life, of a Millennium on earth when justice rules, promises the world's return to its original nature and government: a reformed earthly theocracy. In both scenarios, apocalyptic writing attempts to reveal what is unknown: God's plan for the future. Apocalyptic writings seek to reveal the true but hidden course of history, whether those writings are prophetic utterances, interpretations of earlier revelations, or poems like *Piers Plowman* that reveal the immediate consequences of society's changing values through the language and imagery of earlier revelations.

Langland relies on the eschatological tradition for his model of individual salvation and on the regenerative tradition for his vision of a reformed society. *Piers Plowman*'s agricultural roots and its hopes of holy society on earth clearly belong in the regenerative tradition, and if we consider the poem in this context, its spiraling visions, the dreamer's endless search for Piers, and general lack of closure reflect an understandable predicament rather than clear poetic failure. As Walter W. Skeat argues, the enigmatic ending of *Piers Plowman* may be more satifactory than it seems because it depicts "the very nature of the case,"[1] the very condition of earthly pilgrims and their endless search. As Skeat put the question, "What other ending can there be?" for "the end is not yet. We may be defeated, yet not cast down; we may be dying, and yet live."[2] Until the world is once again a theocracy, until all men live the life of Piers Plowman, Christians, like the poem's wandering dreamer, are always in mid-pilgrimage, and their tribulations and challenges are without end.

But while the poem's vision of society is regenerative, the person of Piers is not only a model for reformed individuals, but "an eschatological figure," as Bloomfield explains. Piers is

> both the way and the goal of Christian perfection. He is both the model and the norm of human existence for Christians, and he can lead them into the transformed society—the Kingdom of God, which may also be an age of the Holy Ghost. He will lead them back so that they may go forward to their proper destiny.[3]

The tension between Piers's eschatological and regenerative significance is precisely that he leads his followers back in order to go forward; the poem suggests that the way contemporary society will move beyond corruption to renew itself is by restoring the order of feudalism and the apostolic integrity of the Church. Langland's figure of the plowman, an ideal representative of the commons, suggests that a return to traditional work will reorder society. The clearly nostalgic figure of the hardworking plowman, who produces food for the common good of all society, reveals a longing for a restored Christian order. This sort of backward vision, a longing for the past expressed as a projection of the future, is what I call radical nostalgia. Nostalgia in this context does not mean sentimentality, but both spiritual longing and a serious emotional attachment to things of the past. In the tradition of Augustine, Will the Dreamer exhibits the condition of the thirsty soul, the hungry or restless heart longing to return home to its source, God.[4] Related to this condition is the pain of mutability and the longing for a permanent home in heaven. In *Piers Plowman*, Langland surveys a disintegrated society and mourns the ruin of the Christian community for which he longs.

Whether we choose to consider Langland a "radical" or not largely depends on which sense of the word we consider. In this study, "radical" is used primarily in its fourteenth-century sense, which according to Raymond Williams, "expressed[ed] an inherent and fundamental quality."[5] Like its Latin source *radix*, meaning "root," the word "radical" not only suggests a fundamentalist return to the perceived basis of society, in this case feudal Christianity, but also points up the agricultural metaphors central to Christianity and to Langland's poem. In the sense that he looks back to the roots of Christian society to find solutions to contemporary problems, Langland practices what we might call "radical apocalypticism." Using the term "radical" to describe Langland's vision of future society is also fitting because the cultural phenomenon that *Piers Plowman* helped to inspire, in which rebels such as John Ball adopted the figure of the plowman, was often revolutionary, transforming Langland's brand of conservative radicalism into the sort of action we would today label as radical.

If we think of apocalypticism as a social myth, as an historical perspective by which one can organize and subsume past and contemporary events to construct a comprehensive narrative involving the future, we can begin to understand how poets like Langland produced apocalyptic writings and how some readers took the social vision and the call for change in *Piers Plowman* seriously enough to transform the allegory of *dowel*, *dobet*, and *dobest* into a program for sometimes violent social action, adapting key terms from the poem and reiterating the pilgrimage to Christian perfection as a contemporary battle of *trewemen* and their oppressors.

Although he questions the generic validity of apocalyptic writing, Morton W. Bloomfield clearly underscores the relationship between reform and apocalyptic thought in Langland's time:

> First of all, the very subject of [*Piers Plowman*], Christian perfection, in its social form, bespeaks apocalypticism. Social thinking on the subject of perfection, above all in the fourteenth century, had to be apocalyptic. The transcendence of society to a new level was thought by many to be the only way out of the crushing dilemmas. The sad state of the contemporary Church could be explained only on these grounds. God was planning, if not a new age, at least a renewal of the good and the just.[6]

But while Bloomfield and later Kathryn Kerby-Fulton[7] focus on Langland's cry for reform of the clergy and the institutional Church, *Piers Plowman* calls for reform of all Christians, religious and secular alike. Langland criticizes not only friars and parish clergy, but courtiers, lawyers, retailers, minstrels, and manual laborers for setting their hearts on earthly instead of heavenly treasure. Regardless of which profession he criticizes, whenever Langland urges moral reform, he urges fiscal reform and a return to traditional Christian attitudes toward economic life.

Not all critics agree that the regenerative and eschatological traditions both survived into the fourteenth century. Considering only the church's official stance, historians such as C. A. Patrides often argue that by the Middle Ages, Christianity succeeded in replacing the more ancient, circular views of history:

> If the meaningless cycles of flux and reflux common to the Greco-Roman attitude toward history are like the legendary phoenix, periodically dying only in order to revive again, to Christians, on the other hand, history is like Jacob's Ladder, leading the Christ-guided pilgrim forever upward in a straight line toward the Eternal City, the Christ being not only present at every point of the ladder but also—as Renaissance commentators frequently observed—the ladder itself.[8]

The problem with such a generalization becomes clear if we reflect on early and medieval Christians' practical experience. For people who usually lived close to the ravages of nature, who planted and harvested according to lunar phases, who followed a religious calendar that repeated annually a cycle of seasons and feasts, a strictly linear view of history flew in the face of experience. Even the actual movement of a pilgrimage, that popular metaphor for one's passage on earth, reinforced the circular paradigm as a means to final salvation. While pilgrims hoped to move straight toward salvation, they visited holy places and, barring death or detour, usually returned home. While the spiritual movement may have been linear, the physical movement was circular. According to medieval Christians such as the twelfth-century Neoplatonists of Chartres and Alain de Lille, even the blessed soul moved in a circle as it returned to God.[9]

One way to illustrate the attempts of early Christians to adapt pagan myths to a linear eschatological view of history is to consider the transformation of the phoenix myth evident in the Exeter Book. N. F. Blake summarizes the development of the phoenix story from an Egyptian creation myth into a Christian allegory. The pagan version of the story associates the phoenix with the sun because of its return and rebirth at the temple at Heliopolis, a city of the sun that features a holy tree, spices and perfumes, and a fountain, lake, or spring.[10] When Lactantius, Gregory, and other Christians such as the Old English poet recount and interpret the phoenix myth, it becomes an allegory of the Final Judgment and the resurrection of the dead.[11]

On one level, the phoenix itself signifies Christ, and the birds who follow him are the righteous saved; at the same time, the phoenix signifies every Christian who builds a nest of good works. One of the reasons the allegory of the Old English *Phoenix* is not consistent is that the poem reiterates the pagan regenerative myth represented by the bird's circular flight at the same time that it asserts a teleological, eschatological interpretation. The imperfect and uneasy transformation of pagan myth into Christian allegory seeks to transform the circular view of history into the linear Christian view of history; but just as Christian poets could not completely alter the pattern of the mythical bird's return, Christian theologians could not destroy the tradition of regeneration. The growing tension between linear and circular models for salvation history, the tension apparent in the Old English *Phoenix,* illustrates the staying power of the regenerative, communal vision.

Pondering two conflicting traditions concerning the pattern of history, Christian writers balanced two apocalyptic traditions that promised two different sorts of perfect community—one rural, one urban. The garden paradise, the heir to pagan tradition and the Old Testament Eden, promised a new cycle of history on earth—a new beginning, while the restored city of Jerusalem, the finally reconstructed homeland, became the site of the end of history. The growing influence of the urban, political, teleological vision correlates with the growing importance of the institutional Church and the urban centers of Europe as hubs of religious and political power, eclipsing the rural vision of restoration that developed from the agricultural metaphors and symbols of the Old and New Testaments. But just as an eclipse does not destroy a heavenly body but only interrupts our ability to see it, the agricultural tradition was not destroyed, but merely overshadowed by the literate, institutional ideology of the powerful forces of Church and State. In an apparent paradox, apocalyptic thought by the Middle Ages presented a view of history that was at once teleological and regenerative: on the one hand, the apocalypse signaled the end of history, destruction, final judgment, and the establishment of the New Jerusalem, a place where the City of God and the City of Man would converge and begin a new phase of heavenly history; on the other hand, the apocalyptic tradition promised regeneration, the *renovatio mundi*. Official church doctrine since before the time of Augustine may have sanctioned a linear view of sacred history, but the regenerative tradition continued to thrive in popular and literary culture. For example, accommodating both views, some Christians awaited the Millennium, which promised a prelapsarian heaven on earth, but only for the thousand years preceding the end of time.

We can learn much about the survival of restorative apocalypticism in the later Middle Ages by considering the prophetic and apocalyptic expressions that informed this tradition, particularly those in the Bible. Subjects of debate from before the time of Jesus, the great battle, the final days, the coming or return of the messiah, and the hope of communal and individual salvation have occupied the minds of generations of Jews and Christians. Sometimes inspired by nationalistic hope, sometimes by spiritual fervor, apocalyptic thought and writing often flourished when God's people believed themselves under siege by evil forces and in need of deliverance, and the abundance of such expressions intensify at the approach of a date of predicted significance, such as A.D. 1000, and during the experience of plague, famine, earthquakes and other natural disasters which appeared to signal the Final Days.

Because of the eschatological visions in the Book of Revelation, readers often assume that all apocalyptic writings are eschatological. A look at older biblical apocalyptic writings, however, reveals calls for change which repeatedly promise restoration of society, often in the form of a restored Jerusalem, and which express no anticipation of the end of history or time. In response to subjugation, war, and displacement, Old Testament apocalyptic writers produce a myth of social redemption in which God repeatedly acts on behalf of a chosen people to vanquish a series of oppressors. Old Testament apocalyptic writing responds to specific historical circumstances in which believers envision victory; such a vision is inherently political, as Norman Cohn points out in a discussion of the Book of Daniel:

> Promises of future compensation for present affliction took on a new tone when theywere directed to the lower strata of the Jewish population as a form of nationalist propaganda. In the apocalypses, poetic imagery of great power not infrequently served the imperious needs of what can only be described as a collective megalomania.[12]

When later beleaguered peoples adopt the apocalyptic imagery of the Old Testament to make sense of their predicaments and to imagine ways out of them, they reiterate and sometimes enact the earlier apocalyptic narratives.

The recurrence of apocalyptic passages in the Old Testament, the expectation of God's direct intervention in history, and the series of Israel's partial or temporary victories suggest a cyclical view of history throughout which God alternately punishes his chosen people for their infidelity and rewards them for their faith. Early cyclical views of history thus include not only pagan extrapolations based on observations of nature, but intepretations of the political and social history of God's people. Patrides asserts that the cyclical paradigm gave way to a linear concept of history even before the early Christian period. He argues that the idea of the end of the world, "involving a universal judgement and the advent of 'new heavens and a new earth,'" came fairly late in Jewish thought, but that "[o]nce this idea became widespread, the Jewish view of history stood complete. In diametric opposition to the Greco-Roman series of purposeless cycles, history was now seen to be linear, progressing in a straight line from the six days of creation to the single Day of Judgement."[13] Patrides points out one obvious exception to the linear representations of history in the Old Testament: the Book of Ecclesiastes. He explains that Ecclesiastes, which he assures us was "obviously the labor of a 'schismatic,'" was later revised and "heroically defended as 'orthodox' by centuries of commentators."[14] Still, he argues, "the extent to which the book departs from the predominant tenor of the Bible is inescapable."[15] This departure is probably related to the book's call for change, its apocalyptic tone; dating from a time after the Exile, the book most likely appeared during a transitional stage in Israel's religious and political development.[16] To illustrate the book's main theme, that all is vanity, the writer of Ecclesiastes contrasts the futile actions and short lives of people with the steady cycles of nature.[17] Later Christian readers could easily regard the various accounts of devastation and restoration in the Old Testament and the renewed promise that God would establish a just society as various expressions of a single hope: a final victory for God's people. For Christians of the early Middle Ages, however, the goal of victory was not only spiritual, but political, culminating in the establishment of the theocracy of the New Jerusalem.

The vision of the Final Judgment in the Book of Revelation not only reveals a New Jerusalem, but promises the vindication of early Christian martyrs and the destruction of the enemies of the Church:

> And I saw seats; and they sat upon them; and the souls of them that were beheaded for the testimony of Jesus, and for the word of God, and who had not adored the beast nor his image, nor received his character on their foreheads, or in their hands; and they lived and reigned with Christ a thousand years.[18]

Composed in the second half of the first century when early Christians suffered Roman persecution, most severely under Nero and Domitian, the Apocalypse, or Book of Revelation, borrows its imagery from the Book of Daniel, another messianic work written in response to persecution.[19] Like Daniel, The Book of Revelation promises a future in which God will avenge his people and the "Son of Man" will establish an eternal kingdom of the elect. Daniel describes his vision, which is not only religious, but political:

> I beheld therefore in the vision of the night, and lo, one like the son of man came with the clouds of heaven, and he came even to the Ancient of days; and they

> presented him before him. And he gave him power, and glory, and a kingdom: and all peoples, tribes and tongues shall serve him: his power is an everlasting power that shall not be taken away: and his kingdom that shall not be destroyed.[20]

For both Israel and the early Christians, apocalyptic writings express a desire for retribution and theocracy, a hope both political and religious.

While the struggles of the Crusades show the continued ideological importance of the earthly city of Jerusalem, their failure, coupled with the growing influence of eschatological thought, transformed the promise of a restored theocracy into the promise of a site of eternal salvation: Heavenly Jerusalem. Norman Cohn discusses the relationship between the restored national home and the heavenly city:

> In the prophecies of the post-exilic period and in the apocalypses the messianic kingdom is imagined as centred on a future Jerusalem which has been rebuilt in great magnificence . . . . Moreover, even for theologians Jerusalem was also a 'figure' or symbol of the heavenly city 'like unto a stone most precious' which according to the Book of Revelation was to replace it at the end of time.[21]

With God as king and his victorious people as its citizenry, the New Jerusalem is transformed from a sacred city into a heavenly one, its people transformed from living believers into the resurrected dead.

Just as God's chosen people were warned to be faithful to God's word in Old Testament apocalyptic writings so that they might deserve the kingdom, Christian apocalyptic writings usually include a call for holy living and moral reform in preparation for final judgment. While evidence in the New Testament makes it clear that Jews during Jesus' time debated whether or not there would be a resurrection of the dead,[22] Jesus clearly preached such a resurrection.[23] According to the Gospel of Matthew, whether one earns a place in the company of the saved or the damned at the Resurrection of the Dead, whether one is among the "chosen" or not, depends on one's works. Jesus describes the Final Judgment, explaining that the Son of Man will come in his glory, assemble people of all nations, separate them one from another as the shepherd separates the sheep from the goats, and then reward the sheep with the kingdom and punish the goats with the everlasting fire prepared for the devil and his angels.[24] This scheme of salvation is dualistic—one is either a sheep or a goat, either saved or damned, good or evil, true or false. Whether one is saved or damned clearly depends on one's actions, for the sheep are rewarded for feeding the hungry, welcoming the stranger, clothing the naked, and visiting the sick and those in prison, while the goats are damned for neglecting such acts of charity.[25] Calls for reform and the dualistic grouping of humanity into good and evil camps are two enduring characteristics of apocalyptic thought. Although Langland expresses anxiety over the presumption involved with making such moral judgments of others,[26] he nonetheless cleaves society in his poem's Prologue into the companies of good and evil, tower and dungeon, Holy Church and Meed, leaving between them the "fair feeld ful of folk"[27] poised for salvation or damnation.

Urgency of tone is another characteristic of most apocalyptic writing. For every apocalyptic group "the time is now," a sentiment shared by Langland and the rebels who use the phrase in their letters, a sentiment that produces the urgency of apocalyptic expression. Jesus and most of the earliest Christians apparently believed that the time of judgment was quickly approaching and that the final days and the messianic kingdom were imminent.[28] From early Christian times, some believers expected warning signs of the Second Coming,[29] while others expected that the Second Coming would come "like a thief."[30] Jesus warned his disciples to be on the alert, promising that "this generation shall not pass, till all these things be done. . . . But of that day and hour no one knoweth, no not the angels of heaven, but the Father alone."[31] Still, apocalyptic thinkers consistently watch for signs of the end times and often find them in their own historical circustances, thus fueling their sense of urgency.

When the anticipated end did not come as expected, the Apostles and their followers had to explain why. The Christian debate over just when the final days would occur began in the Gospels and Epistles, continued through the early Church, and became an important question for orthodox medieval theologians and heretics alike. Each time a projected date for the Second Coming passed, believers revised their calculations or reinterpreted the scriptures.[32] In this sense, apocalypticism depends on a way of reading in which believers apply the apocalyptic narrative—the anticipated great battle between good and evil and the resulting establishment of just society—to their own social and historical contexts.

The regenerative and eschatological apocalyptic traditions of transformed, ideal society produced two images of paradise: the garden and the kingdom, respectively. The garden, a prelapsarian restoration of peace and plenty not only among nations but between people and animals, humans and nature, features redeemed creation returning full circle to its original, perfect order.[33] The kingdom, no longer a restored national homeland but a heavenly city, represents the culmination of history as Christian society becomes one with heavenly society. Salvation is both individual and social; while individuals are redeemed, society and the nature enjoy the *renovatio mundi.* In each account, salvation is both spiritual and physical; this is no salvation of disembodied souls, but of individuals "new" in body and in spirit.

Before Augustine, Christian expectations for the Millennium easily combined the traditions of the kingdom and the garden. Belief in the resurrection of the dead and chiliastic faith, the belief that Christ would return bodily to establish a millennial rule on earth, were orthodox according to Irenaeus (c. A.D.120–150), bishop of Lyons. Irenaeus, whom Cohn estimates "probably did more than anyone to establish chiliasm in the West," anthologized millennial and messianic prophecies from the Bible and early Christian writings in his treatise *Adversus haereses*.[34] But although Irenaeus expected Christ's kingdom on earth as the final chapter of earth's history, he also recognized that the Millennium would restore creation.[35]

Likewise, Lactantius had little difficulty asserting both traditions in the fourth century. Incorporating both prelapsarian fecundity and classical images of the Golden Age into his apocalyptic vision, Lactantius awaits a victorious king who will judge the living and the dead, reign with the blessed, and found the Holy City of the Millennium, but he describes the abundance of the kingdom in terms of nature's return to its prelapsarian state:

> Throughout that time the stars shall be brighter, and the brightness of the sun shall be increased, and the moon shall not wane. Then the blessing shall descend from God morning and evening, and the earth shall bear all fruits without man's labour. Honey in abundance shall drip from the rocks, fountains of milk and wine shall burst forth. The beasts of the forests shall put away their wildness and become tame . . . no longer shall any animal live by bloodshed. For God shall supply all with abundant and guiltless food.[36]

In such a vision, linear history comes full circle and the world returns to its original condition, in which work is unnecessary, the wolf lies down with the lamb, and peace prevails in the kingdom of God.[37]

As the Church grew into a powerful institution, however, the predominant image of paradise and the chiliastic tradition itself shifted. Origen, in the third century, was one of the first to try to discredit the chiliastic tradition, explaining that the kingdom would not actually be established as a place on earth, but would be constructed in the souls of believers.[38] The Kingdom of God, the

Church itself according to Augustine, had already been established on earth by Christ. In his commentary on the Sermon on the Mount, Augustine explains Matthew 6:10 as follows:

> "Thy kingdom come,". . . is to be understood as meaning "May Thy kingdom be made manifest to men." Just as a light that is present is absent to those who are blind or who shut their eyes, so also the kingdom of God—although it never departs from the earth—is absent to those who know it not. But no one will be allowed to be ignorant of the kingdom of God when—to judge the living and the dead—His Only Begotten Son will have come from heaven, not merely in a manner recognizable by the intellect, but even visibly in the person of the Lord.[39]

No longer was the Kingdom of God only in the future; it lay largely concealed, manifest on this earth but visible only to believers.

In *The City of God*, which R. E. Kaske reminds us became a popular subject of commentaries in the fourteenth century,[40] Augustine proposes that the historical courses of two metaphorical cities, the heavenly city and the earthly city, intersect throughout time. Those who live in the earthly city make false sacrifices, while those who live in the heavenly city are like faithful pilgrims or wayfarers on earth.[41] The heavenly city of *The City of God* coexists with the earthly one, and those who live in both cities make use of temporal goods and suffer temporal ills. They differ in their faith, hope, and love, but will continue to live together until the final judgment.[42] Peter Brown describes the dualistic model that developed:

> Since the Fall of Adam, the human race had always been divided into two great 'cities,' *civitates*; that is, into two great pyramids of loyalty. The one 'city' served God along with His loyal angels; the other served the rebel angels, the Devil and his demons. Although the two 'cities' seemed inextricably mixed, within the church as in the world, they would be separated at the Last Judgement. Christ would speak the words of judgement; the two cities—Babylon and Jerusalem—would then appear plainly, the one on the left, the other on the right.[43]

Augustine depicts the sheep and goats of the Gospels, the saved and the damned, as citizens of Jerusalem and Babylon, respectively. Distinguishing between the resurrection of the spirit and the resurrection of the body, Augustine asserts that the resurrection of the spirit—the salvation of the soul and the promise of everlasting life—can be accomplished on earth by receiving the life of Christ.[44] Affirming the orthodoxy of the resurrection of the body as well, Augustine explains that all bodies will come forth from their graves, and like the sheep and goats of the Gospels, the living dead will be divided according to their deeds.[45] Not all, however, will have earned eternal life, and those who lived badly will rise to eternal death instead of eternal life.[46]

Because Augustine believed that the Church was already living in the Millennium, and because death, disease, sin, and need still obviously plagued the living, the vision of a regenerated earth faded. The restored, edenic world disappears in Augustine's approach to the apocalyptic. Regeneration is not for the Millennium, but for the Final Judgment:

> For the true health of bodies which is awaited from the Lord will be in the end at the resurrection of the dead. Then what will live will not die; then what will be healed will not become ill; then what will be filled will not hunger or thirst; then what will be renewed will not grow old.[47]

Augustine interiorized eschatology. No longer were the Final Days and the end of time historical events perhaps far in the future; the Final Days were always near for perishable humanity.[48] According to Cohn, Augustine's assertions that the Church was already living in the Millennium and that the Book of Revelation was a spiritual allegory rather than a book of historical prophecy "at once became orthodox doctrine, and so definitively that in 431 the Council of Ephesus condemned belief in the Millennium as a superstitious aberration."[49]

Whether the Church sanctioned belief in the Millennium or not, it was unable to counteract the apocalyptic fervor and beliefs of the masses, which it found easier to harness than to eliminate: fears of judgment as 1000 A.D. approached provided an excellent opportunity to encourage devotion and moral reform; the vision of a restored Jerusalem provided motivation for the Crusades; and the construction of the cathedrals offered Christians an opportunity to atone for sins and help build God's kingdom on earth. But even if the growing Church abandoned the regenerative tradition for a more linear, eschatological concept of history, one that began with creation and ended with judgment and the establishment of the Kingdom, it was unable to interrupt the cyclical pattern of history and living manifest in religious and popular culture: in the Church's calendar of yearly feasts, the Neoplatonic journey of the soul, agricultural life, the Cycle Plays, the Wheel of Fortune.

Augustine, in his attempts to discredit the pagan cyclical view of history, surely never expected that *The City of God* would encourage the Christian Neoplatonists of twelfth-century Chartres to reintegrate pagan views of history into religious and literary culture. Platonic idealism complemented Augustine's idea of simultaneous cities of God and man—one perfect, one imperfect, coexisting and sometimes converging—and Platonic notions of macrocosm and microcosm provided a link between the two. In addition, Plato's description in the *Timaeus* of a creator who is both craftsman and father corresponded well with Christian beliefs about the Creator. Plato, who had been able to reach conclusions so similar to Christian beliefs by observing nature and employing philosophical argument,[50] remained an authority throughout the Middle Ages, and his ideas helped to repopularize the cyclical view of history and to reinforce Augustinian dualism.[51]

The first third of the *Timaeus* was the only text of Plato's known directly in the twelfth-century West, but while medieval Christians might not have known the entire *Timaeus* or any other of Plato's works directly, numerous commentaries and summaries were available. Winthrop Wetherbee lists several medieval sources for information on the *Timaeus*, including a commentary by Calcidius, Martianus's *De nuptiis*, Macrobius's commentary on the *Somnium Scipionis*, and various philosophical treatises.[52] In addition, Boethius summarized the cosmology of the *Timaeus* in the prayer *O Qui perpetua*, Thierry worked to reconcile Plato and *Genesis*, and Guillaume de Conches wrote a commentary on the *Timaeus*.[53]

In the *Timaeus*, Plato describes the cyclical journey of the soul from its heavenly birthplace, to purification on earth, and back to its origin. This movement is analogous to the journey of the Christian phoenix; both the Christian phoenix and the Platonic soul undergo purification in preparation for their return to their heavenly sources. By contrast, the earlier pagan phoenix myths promised a return to earth after immolation and purification. Wetherbee points out that while earlier Christians such as Origen criticized Plato's concept of the journey of the soul, claiming that it promised salvation for all, in the twelfth century this idea, modified, regained popularity; in his glosses on Plato, Guillaume de Conches justified the Platonic view, explaining that only sufficiently pure souls could make the journey.[54]

An important influence on the Chartrian Neoplatonists and on literary tradition, Boethius also asserted cyclical history and cosmology. Chaucer's translation of the *Consolation of Philosophy*, for instance, provides us with a fine example of Neoplatonic thought in fourteenth-century English:

> Alle thynges seken ayen to hir propre cours, and alle thynges rejoysen hem of hir retornynge ayen to hir nature. Ne noon ordenaunce is bytaken to thynges, but that that hath joyned the endynge to the bygynnynge, and hath maked the course of itself stable (that it chaunge nat from his propre kynde).[55]

Influencing not only Chaucer, but Jean de Meun and Alain de Lille before him, Boethius spread Neoplatonic cosmological and historical concepts.[56]

In addition to its philosophical influence, the *Consolation of Philosophy* helped popularize generic features common to both apocalyptic literature and dream-vision poetry. Kathryn Kerby-Fulton lists some of the conventions of apocalyptic writing apparent in *Piers Plowman*, including "an apparent lack of surface cohesion, a particular brand of self-deprecating autobiographical visionary stance, and a shifting use of allegorical imagery,"[57] all of which are generic features not only of apocalyptic literature, but of medieval dream-vision poetry. The same holds true of other features of dream-vision poetry noted by A. C. Spearing, which include "an ideal and often symbolic landscape, in which the dreamer encounters an authoritative figure, from whom he learns some religious or secular doctrine."[58] With so many generic features in common, John's Apocalypse, Boethius's *Consolation of Philosophy*, Alain de Lille's *Complaint of Nature*, and Langland's poem, among others,[59] illustrate the close relationship between apocalypses and dream-vision poems. Not only in terms of philosophy but of framework, the influence of Boethius and the Chartrian Neoplatonists on the dream-vision poetry of fourteenth-century England indicates the enduring popularity of visionary and regenerative ideology.

By the second half of the Middle Ages, cyclical and linear representations of history coexisted, reflecting the coexistence of Neoplatonic and eschatological thought. Although cyclical conceptions of nature and history grew in popularity, the later Middle Ages also experienced burgeoning eschatological belief. As Cohn points out, the Calabrian hermit Joachim of Fiore (1145–1202) was instrumental in popularizing eschatology as prophecy. Cohn explains that while "allegorical and typological interpretation had always played a large part in traditional patristic exegesis," and while "the idea that the Scriptures possessed a concealed meaning was far from new, " Joachim was an innovator in that now "these methods could be applied not simply for moral or dogmatic purposes but as a means of understanding and forecasting the development of history."[60] Apocalyptic expression as prophetic articulation was, of course, not altogether new, but new for Christian thinkers who no longer read books such as Daniel in their original historical context. Instead, Joachim read apocalyptic and prophetic scripture in its contemporary context, applying the imagery and typology of eschatology to the present and the future and preparing the way for the millenarian movements of the later Middle Ages. Apocalyptic writings were no longer mere historical relics, but prophetic projections of the past. As Marjorie Reeves explains, millenarian groups usually maintained that their beliefs "sprang from a myth of the future—not the past,"[61] but they also depended on models of the past to envision their ideal future. Their understanding of history "enabled [millenarian groups] to complete the pattern of things to come in the Last Age and to find their own cosmic role within this pattern."[62] By asserting the relationship between past and future events, Joachim was able to offer a compromise between the cyclical and linear views of history: the spiral. Reeves explains Joachim's spiral view of history:

> Year by year the Church keeps the round of liturgy, yet all the time she is tending towards her goal. So in a complex spiralling diagram of the religious seasons and the lectionary Joachim traces her course until it issues in the triumphant spiral which represents the time between Easter and Pentecost . . . . At Pentecost the end of the spiral takes the Church into the Eighth Day of eternal bliss. It is an ironical testimony to the subconscious associations touched off by shapes that, because this figure was coiled round in a spiral with a tail, Joachim's disciples added a wicked serpent's head and transformed it into an incongruous symbol of evil.[63]

While the snake's length signifies the larger course of history, the unfolding of time, its coils represent each age, each revolution. The serpent of history also measures the course of time, a course that began with the snake in the garden and would end with the serpent being crushed.[64] Joachim thus accommodates the linear and cyclical paradigms, the eschatological and the apocalyptic, by envisioning history as a series of coils in a larger framework of progress toward God and holy society.

Further encouraging eschatological and apocalyptic ideas, Joachim reintroduced the idea that the Millennium, the "Third Age" in his historical scheme, was yet to come, an idea that had been discredited since Augustine. As Cohn notes, the Papacy's sponsorship of Joachim "sanction[ed] a new form of that chiliasm which for centuries it had been condemning as heretical."[65] By Joachim's time, current events and politics had once again become signs of eschatological import, incidents in part of a larger apocalyptic drama. One such marriage of eschatology and politics apparent throughout the Middle Ages is the apocalyptic motif we might call the "return of the King." Like Christ, a whole series of local and national saviors, from Constantine to Charlemagne to Arthur, were expected to return, and were sometimes even sighted by believers.[66] While some of these heroes were expected to rise from the dead, others were believed to be only sleeping. A popular motif, the pattern of the sleeping or dead hero waiting to return and rule, also arose in England, where Arthur was thought by some to wait on the Isle of Avalon. Such popular adaptations of chiliastic expectation show how closely allied history, literature, and millenarianism had become. All the later Middle Ages needed was a series of crises—plague, economic upheaval, and political and religious corruption—to provoke contemporary apocalyptic expressions.

While some Christians of the later Middle Ages awaited the reformed society of the Millennium or the Third Age, others still interiorized eschatology in the Augustinian tradition. We can see this tendency in *Pearl*, where the New Jerusalem is not still to be established on earth, but already established in heaven as the City of God. The vision of New Jerusalem in *Pearl* is no apocalyptic vision of the future, but a dream vision of the city of the afterlife. The maiden in *Pearl* makes a distinction between the earthly and the heavenly, between old Jerusalem, in Judea, and the New Jerusalem:

Þat is þe cyte þat þe Lombe con fonde
To soffer inne sor for manez sake,
Þe olde Jerusalem to understonde,
For þere þe olde gulte watz don to slake.
Bot þe nwe, þat lyȝt of Godez sonde,
Þe apostel in Apocalyppce in theme con take,
Þe Lombe þer withouten spottez blake
Hatz feryed þyder Hys fayre flote;
And as Hys flok is withouten flake,
So is Hys mote withouten moote.[67]

The New Jerusalem is already populated with spotless Christians whom the vision transforms into perfect jewels, like Pearl herself. The dreamer tells us that he saw the holy city just as John described it, remarking that he only knew the names of the precious stones because they were recorded in the Apocalypse.

The New Jerusalem of *Pearl* is not, however, the only depiction of paradise in the poem. The *Pearl* poet distinguishes not only between the earthly and heavenly cities, but between earthly and heavenly gardens as well. The unnatural landscape of the dream-vision, with its silver trees, crystal cliffs, and pearl gravel, appears as a space between the earth and New Jerusalem.[68] This transformed, ideal landscape, which Andrew and Waldron call the "Terrestrial Paradise," combines the apocalyptic Christian tradition and the pagan tradition, the landscape of Revelations and the pagan *locus amoenus*.[69] With its beautiful trees, flowers, singing birds, shimmering lights, and swirling water, the place is transformed, but recognizable. No longer the earthly terrestrial paradise of the Millennium, the Terrestrial Paradise of *Pearl* does not await an earthly *renovatio*, but is the borderland of heaven, a marginal countryside through which one passes to arrive at the glittering city, the New Jerusalem.

By contrast, the first garden of the poem is an earthly *locus amoenus*, a sweet-smelling expanse of turf that leads to a grave. While the New Jerusalem is eternal and the Terrestrial Paradise is not corruptible, life in the green garden of earth is decidedly transient. Although the Christian hopes for salvation and eternal life, he or she is subject to the cycles of nature, the earthly patterns of seasons and plantings, the reality of death and the promise of rebirth. As the mourner wanders through the green garden at harvest time toward the maiden's grave, he thinks of his Pearl rolling away and buried beneath the earth:

> To þat spot þat I in speche expoun
> I entred in þat erber grene,
> In Augoste in a hyȝ seysoun,
> Quen corne is coruen wyth crokez kene.
> On huyle þer perle hit trendeled doun
> Schadowed þis wortez ful schyre and schene:
> Gilofre, gyngure, and gromylyoun,
> And pyonys powdered ay bytwene.
> ȝif hit watz semly on to sene,
> Þer wonys þat worþyly, I wot and wene,
> My precious perle wythouten spot.[70]

The analogies between harvest and death and between the seed in the field and the maiden in the grave promise new life, the resurrection of the dead, from what is buried in the ground:

Flor and fryte may not be fede
Þer hit doun drof in moldez dunne,
For vch gresse mot grow of graynez dede;
No whete were ellez to wonex wonne.
Of o goud vche goude is ay bygonne:
So semly a sede moȝt fayly not,
Þat spryngande spycez vp ne sponne
Of þat precios perle wythouten spotte.[71]

The dying of plants to produce seeds, and from them new life, reflects a long tradition of agricultural metaphors for both the individual eschatology of death and the social transformation of apocalypse.[72] For society, the harvest is the Final Judgment; for the individual, the harvest signifies the moment of judgment at death, when one begins to reap the rewards or suffer the punishments of one's works on earth. The more one plants and tends, the greater is the harvest, just as the more good works one does, the greater is one's heavenly reward; the success or failure of the harvest thus measures the quality and quantity of work and works. The relationship between labor and reward, between works and salvation, is central to a study of late medieval apocalypticism. Chapter Two more fully explores the economics of salvation, a subject especially significant for a study of *Piers Plowman*.

CHAPTER TWO

Economics and Salvation:
Paying for Sin and Reaping Reward

For medieval Christians, economic discourse and religious discourse were inseparable. On the one hand, economic metaphors such as redemption, satisfaction, and sacrifice dominated medieval discussions of penance and salvation; on the other hand, the Church tried to govern economic life by providing guidelines for ethical economic interaction. James Simpson notes that Langland "consistently uses economic imagery to describe spiritual relations" and that Langland's economic language is often "drawn from the terms of a *profit* economy."[1] For Langland, economic and religious reform were inseparable; for example, his baldly economic expression, "Pay what you owe" is both a moral and economic dictum.[2]

Morton W. Bloomfield identifies *redde quod debes* as a principle central to understanding *Piers Plowman* and Langland's ideas about justice and salvation:

> *Redde quod debes* is a recurrent theme of the Do-best section, is the essence of Truth's pardon in Passus VII, and is a central point in the confession of Avarice in Passus V. . . . I believe it is a basic feature of Langland's political and social thought and a key to one of the meanings of the poem.[3]

Ensuring not only economic justice but forgiveness for sins, proper restitution benefits both the wronged party and the sinner, providing compensation for material loss and for sins, respectively. Bloomfield stresses the principle's role as the means to both individual salvation and social reform: "Christian perfection must in part, if not fundamentally, be social, and hence must involve action. Justice, as summed up in *redde quod debes*, is Christianity in action."[4]

In *Piers Plowman*, Christian perfection, both individual and societal, depends on action. The progression in *Piers Plowman* from *dowel* to *dobet* to *dobest*, each of which requires greater social action on the part of the Christian, ensures justice and promises the establishment of millennial society. *Redde quod debes* is thus a means to perfect Christian society in *Piers Plowman*; for example, in the apocalyptic conclusion of the B-text, the community entrenched in the barn *Unitas,* representing Holy Church, waits for Conscience to pay what he owes, to receive a proper penance so that restitution is made and a perfect, just Christian society established; however, instead of confessing to honest clergy for a properly severe punishment, Conscience receives his penance from the Antichrist friar. The friar gives him a penance too lenient to constitute restitution, frustrates justice and the establishment of perfect Christian society, and provokes Conscience into beginning a new pilgrimage to find Piers.

But while *redde quod debes* is a principle of justice or law and an imperative for the establishment of millennial society, it is also an economic principle. Jacques Le Goff examines the growing link between economic and religious life in the later Middle Ages and notes the growing importance of economic life in the eschatological scheme: "It was during the thirteenth century that thinkers turned work into the basis of wealth and salvation, both on the eschatological level and on what we might call the economic level."[5] The penalties sinners "pay" for sins and the rewards faithful Christians expect to reap are part of a series of exchanges carrying both religious and economic weight.

Discussing the sacrament of penance without economic metaphors is almost impossible; for example, the sacrament requires satisfaction, that sinners pay what they owe for their transgressions in order to redeem their souls. Those who do not make restitution during their lifetimes will pay for their transgressions in purgatory or hell and on Judgment Day. Following his granting Piers and his company the authority to forgive sins if the principle *redde quod debes* is met, Jesus ascends and waits to judge according to the same principle:

> Anoon after an heigh vp into heuene
> He wente, and wonye þere, and wil come at þe last
> and reward hym right wel þat *reddit quod debet*,
> Paie parfitly as pure truþe wold.
> And what persone paieþ it nouȝt punysshen he þenkeþ,
> And demen hem at domesday, boþe quyke and dede,
> The goode to godhede and to greet Ioye,
> and wikkede to wonye in wo wiþouten ende.[6]

The measure by which all forgiveness is granted, paying what one owes ensures eternal salvation.

When Langland repeats "Pay what you owe," he uses the economic metaphor to imply that mere monetary payments are inadequate for those who seek redemption; Christians owe not only the product of their labor, but work itself. When Langland speaks of what one "owes," he speaks not only of reparation for sins, but of social obligations, and because religious and social obligations depend on *status*, Langland fuses feudal work and Christian works, as Lawrence M. Clopper notes:

> Langland's rather pragmatic scheme of salvation depends as much on fulfilling the occupation to which one has been called as it does on Christian belief; in order to avoid spiritual indebtedness, a person must know precisely his calling because only by knowing his calling can he determine his obligations to others and therefore to God.[7]

Individuals can earn salvation by doing their proper work, and working as true Christians—i.e., honestly—will restore society. From the very beginning of *Piers Plowman*, Langland suggests that the renovation of Christian society depends on a return to proper economic relations as defined by feudal obligation and moral responsibility, such as providing for the poor. A kingdom in which all people of every *status* work according to each estate's obligations, perfect Christian society and justice hinge on the restoration of feudal categories. In the Prologue to *Piers Plowman,* Langland offers a vision of such a utopia:

> Thanne kam þer a kyng; knyȝthod hym ladde;
> Might of þe communes made hym to regne.
> And þanne cam kynde wit and clerkes he made
> For to counseillen þe kyng and þe commune saue.
> The kyng and knyȝthod and clergie boþe
> Casten þat þe commune sholde hire communes fynde.
> The commune contreued of kynde wit craftes,
> And for profit of al þe peple Plowmen ordeyned
> To tilie and to trauaille as trewe lif askeþ.
> The kyng and þe commune and kynde wit þe þridde
> Shopen lawe and leaute, ech lif to knowe his owene.[8]

In this ideal vision of feudal life, knights protect, clergy counsels, and commons toil all for the benefit of the community.[9] This exemplary community, however, bears little resemblance to the chaotic and corrupt kingdom whose description immediately precedes it in the poem. When the poet's attention shifts back from the ideal court to the contemporary one, references to the political discontent and economic upheavals of contemporary society come streaming into the poem along with the "route of Ratons."[10]

Langland's panoramic vision of contemporary society in the Prologue displays a community in crisis, threatened by corruption and conspicuous consumption, its members poised between disaster and victory, between the tower and the dungeon. When Langland attempts to describe this society according to the tri-partite estate model, not all people fit in to the scheme or are working as they should:

> A fair feeld ful of folk fond I þer bitwene
> Of alle manere of men, þe meene and þe riche,
> Werchyng and wandrynge as þe world askeþ.
> Some putten hem to plouȝ, pleiden ful selde,
> In settynge and sowynge swonken ful harde;
> Wonnen þat þise wastours with glotonye destruyeþ.
> And somme putten hem to pride, apparailed hem þerafter.
> In contenaunce of cloþynge comen disgised.
> In preieres and penaunce putten hem manye,
> Al for loue of oure lord lyueden wel streyte
> In hope for to haue heueneriche blisse.
> As Ancres and heremites þat holden hem in hire selles,
> Coueiten noȝt in contree to cairen aboute
> For no likerous liflode hire likame to plese.
> And somme chosen hem to chaffare; þei cheueden þe bettre,
> As it semeþ to our siȝt þat swiche men þryueþ.[11]

Casting suspicion on such devotion to commercial professions, Langland emphasizes volition by using two forms of the verb "to choose" in line 31 of the Prologue. For Langland, those in business were not born to their work in the same way that others were born into their customary vocations, but actively chose to abjure their proper work in order to obtain wealth. Juxtaposed with ascetic anchorites, those who choose to work for earthly instead of heavenly profit store up their treasures here on earth instead of storing it in heaven. Merchants and others in commerce may seem to thrive in terms of material standards, to human eyes; in the eyes of God, however, they may be in grave danger, as Langland warns elsewhere:

For many men on þis moolde moore setten hir herte
In good þan in god; forþi hem grace failleþ[12]

If we note that the gifts Grace distributes in Passus XIX are the traditional occupations, we see the poem's link between spiritual grace and exercising one's traditional vocation. Grace fails those who pursue material goods in the new market economy, those who ignore Grace's vocational gift to make a profit.

Infected by *wastours,* conspicuous consumers, and merchants, the society corrupted by money and consumption in the Prologue of *Piers Plowman* presents an accumulation of gluttonous beggars, travelling hermits who refuse to work, friars who let lords buy forgiveness, a rogue pardoner who shares the poor's silver with a parish priest, parsons who leave their congregations for London to make money, and other clergy who work for the court:

Somme seruen þe kyng and his siluer tellen,
In Cheker and in Chauncelrie chalangen hise dettes
Of wardes and of wardemotes, weyues and streyves.
And somme seruen as seruauntȝ lordes and ladies,
And in stede of Stywardes sitten and demen.[13]

Instead of being stewards of their parishes and protectors of the poor and orphaned, these members of the clergy work "in stede" of stewards for lords, as overseers. Counting silver like Judas, servants of lords and ladies instead of servants of the poor, such clerics betray God as they sit and *demen*, a verb that calls to mind their making judgments against the poor in favor of the lords for whom they work as well as their eventually being judged for betraying their vocations.

A chief cause of injustice in the world of *Piers Plowman*, a society in which confessors accept payments to absolve the wealthy for cheating or otherwise abusing the poor, is the blurred distinction between the metaphors of payment that dominated penitential language and actual monetary payoffs that resulted in practices contrary to Christian faith and tradition, for the selling of sacraments and offices is clearly forbidden by Peter in his rebuke of Simon Magus.[14] For Langland, the alliance of the clergy with the rich instead of with Holy Church is the root of society's moral crises, the cause of the "mooste meschief on

Molde,"[15] for the clergy thus neglects its corrective role in society—its power to rebuke nobles, to hold the wealthy accountable for their actions, and to demand restitution for the injured poor as a condition of forgiveness in the sacrament of penance. In a description reminiscent of Chaucer's portrait of the Monk in the General Prologue to the *Canterbury Tales*, Langland portrays clergy who like to live as lords and who scorn the poor:

> Ac now is Religioun a rydere, a rennere by stretes,
> A ledere of louedayes and a lond buggere,
> A prikere on a palfrey fro place to Manere,
> An heep of houndes at his ers as he a lord were,
> And but his knaue knele þat shal his coppe brynge
> He loureþ on hym and lakkeþ hym: who lered hym curteisie?
> Litel hadde lordes to doon to ȝyue lond from hire heires
> To Religiouse þat han no rouþe þouȝ it reyne on hir Auters.
> In many places þer þei persons ben, be þei purely at ese,
> Of þe pouere haue þei no pite, and þat is hir pure chartre;
> Ac þei leten hem as lordes, hire lond liþ so brode.[16]

Here Langland condemns both the active corruption of lordly clerics and their passive corruption, visible in their indifference to the poor. This passage suggests that the reason for such social climbing among the clergy is the property they have been willed by lords, which does a double harm by corrupting the clergy and disinheriting rightful heirs. As Chapter 3 of this study details more fully, the practice of bequeathing land to the Church became more and more common from the time of the plague as part of the general concentration of wealth that benefitted the Church, merchants, urban consumers, and some prosperous lords at the expense of the rural economy.

Perhaps most vilified among the clergy in *Piers Plowman* are the friars. Langland describes the friars, who "coueitise of copes"[17] gloss the gospels however they see fit and sell forgiveness whenever possible, with apocalyptic urgency:

> Manye of þise maistres mowe cloþen hem at likyng
> For hire moneie and hire marchaundiȝe marchen togideres.
> Siþ charite haþ ben chapman and chief to shryue lordes
> Manye ferlies han fallen in a fewe yeres.

> But holy chirche and hij holde bettre togidres
> The moost meschief on Molde is mountynge vp faste.[18]

At the conclusion of the B-text, when Friar Flattery and his fellow, "sire *Penetrans domos*," are let into the barn of *Unitee*, we see how avaricious friars betray their proper work for profit. When Peace, the porter, asks the friar why he wants to enter, the friar replies that he wants to speak with Contrition "In faiþ . . . for profit and for helþe."[19] If the friar's words were sincere, as Peace assumes, this message would be straightforward, but the antichrist friar's statement misleads in the same way that a friar's *glosed* Gospel can. The friar's words are true but twisted, for the friar and his fellow are not there for the profit of Contrition or Conscience, but for their own profit. Like the friars in the Prologue who store up earthly treasures such as luxurious clothing, these friars not only neglect to store up heavenly treasures for themselves, but, even worse, seduce the same sinners they should be saving into committing more and greater sins by offering easy penance. Instead of a stinging plaster of penance for wounded Contrition, the friar gives him a plaster

> Of 'a pryuee paiement and I shal praye for yow
> And for hem þat ye ben holden to al my lif tyme,
> And make of yow *memoria* in masse and in matyns
> As freres of oure Fraternytee, for a litel siluer'.[20]

The payoff soothes Contrition, "þe souerayne salue for alle synnes of kynde,"[21] who leaves and then lies "enchaunted" and drugged by the friar's remedy so that men fear no sin; the friar is then free to "gooþ and gadereþ and gloseþ þere he shryueþ."[22] This crisis impels the final action of the poem, Conscience's pilgrimage to find Piers, which leaves Christians like Will and society as a whole in the same precarious position that they were in the poem's Prologue. In the context of sacred history, medieval Christian society experienced the same phase of history that Christianity always endures, the period of trials still underway between Pentecost and the Second Coming.

Langland has good reason to depict the Antichrist who enters Unity as a confessor friar. Lester Little notes that the friars' administration of the sacrament of penance was instrumental in popularizing economic language and metaphors that reflected the growing commercial economy, explaining that "the friars further reflected the society they entered by their frequent use of a marketplace vocabulary, a practice that gained authority and impetus from that one-time cloth merchant, Francis of Assisi."[23] The friars' practice of granting indulgences for cash payments, a practice Langland firmly condemns, further illustrates the embedded nature of religious and economic discourse. Little provides a summary of one friar's description of the system of indulgences which reveals the economic exchanges implicit in the practice:

> [A] Dominican writer explained the system of indulgences which came into more frequent use around 1230, as transactions with the church's Treasury of Merits. For a cash payment the penitent person could get credit against his penitential debt from the store of supplemental merit and good works on deposit there from the lives of Christ, Mary, and the saints. From such examples we can see that the friars employed an idiom that was unmistakably urban, just as their behaviour reflected, in a formal sense, the behaviour of the urban professions.[24]

Urban in origin, this commercial vocabulary reflects not only the growth of the friars, but the growth of city schools and the interests of the scholastics. Little notes that by the end of the twelfth century, friars and scholars had started to discuss economic problems including "private property, fair prices, money, professional fees, commercial profits, business partnerships, and moneylending."[25] Challenging traditional attitudes toward such economic subjects, the friars "came up with generally favourable, approving views"[26] of economic life which helped legitimize commercial occupations.

When the *pauperes Christi* adopted the urban vocabulary of the growing market economy, they also hastened the transformation of the traditional economic metaphors of redemption and satisfaction into a market vocabulary in which forgiveness was seemingly bought and sold. Such transactions usually neglected or were at the expense of the poor, particularly the rural poor, for as Chapter 3 details, urban dwellers were in much better financial positions to make monetary contributions in return for a lax penance from a confessor or an indulgence than were rural inhabitants, who were generally shorter on cash.

In a time of increasing monetary wealth, the practice of substituting a monetary payment to a confessor in place of satisfaction that demanded personal action, such as restitution or acts of mercy toward the poor, apparently grew among clergy and wealthy sinners, and changes in religious doctrine and administration of the sacrament of penance in the second half of the Middle Ages made such abuses possible, if not likely. No longer simply charged with assigning the appropriate penance for a particular sin from a handbook, confessors were free to consider a sinner's intentions and then to use their discretion in determining proper penalties.[27] Le Goff compares the manuals, which "focused upon the acts, not upon the actors,"[28] to the growing focus on the sinner and his intentions in the second half of the Middle Ages, explaining that between the late eleventh and the early thirteenth century, "the concept of sin and penance changed profoundly, became spiritualized and internalized. The gravity of a sin was henceforth measured in terms of the sinner's intention. It was therefore necessary to determine whether this intention was good or bad."[29] As confessors delved into sinners' consciences to determine their intentions and thus the gravity of sins, they also considered proper restitution, and for clergy willing to accept payments, such deliberations could become similar to business negotiations; at the same time, intention became important in business as well as in the confessional. Little, for example, reports that the schoolmen "would not justify a merchant, however honest, whose purpose was to accumulate riches," but would judge him guilty of avarice.[30] The schoolmen condoned only an honest merchant "who sought only a modest profit in order to serve his immediate needs and those of his family."[31] A sinful act committed *in extremis*, such as a desperate poor man stealing bread for his family, would be easily forgiven, while the rich man stealing to increase his wealth would warrant stern correction and penance.

The clergy's subjective rather than objective administration of individual penances placed a greater emphasis on the redemptive power of Christian works and helped elevate the status of work in general. No longer merely a post-lapsarian penalty, work and works became central to salvation, as Le Goff explains:

> Medieval man initially viewed labor as a penance or a chastisement for original sin. Then, without abandoning this penitential perspective, they place [*sic*] increasing value upon work as an instrument of redemption, of dignity, of salvation. They viewed labor as collaboration in the work of the Creator who, having labored, rested on the seventh day. Labor, that cherished burden, had to be wrenched from the outcast position and transformed, individually and collectively, into the rocky path to liberation.[32]

Eventually expressed in the Protestant work ethic, the growing emphasis on work and works as a means to salvation was problematic for a faith in which the crucifixion was believed to have already redeemed all baptized believers who chose to follow Christ. In *Piers Plowman*, when Will argues with Scripture, using Peter as an authority that whoever is baptized, whether rich or poor, is saved, Scripture points out that the sort of baptism Peter meant was *in extremis*, and applies only to those who are newly baptized at the point of death. For Christians, however, God ordains a whole different set of expectations and responsibilities:

> Ac cristene men wiþoute moore maye noȝt come to heuene,
> For þat crist for cristene men deide, and confermed þe law
> That whoso wolde and wilneþ wiþ crist to arise . . .
> He sholde louye and lene and þe lawe fulfille.
> That is, loue þi lord god leuest abouen alle,
> And after alle cristene creatures, in commune ech man ooþer;
> And þus bilongeþ to louye þat leueþ to be saued.
> And but we do þus in dede, er þe day of dome,
> It shal bisitten vs ful soure þe siluer þat we kepen,
> And our bakkes þat moþeeten be and seen beggeris go naked,
> Or delit in wyn and wildefowel and wite any in defaute.[33]

Here Langland echoes an apocalyptic passage in the Letter of James that promises justice for laborers and the poor along with punishment for those who neglect or abuse them when the husbandman who waits for the fruits of the earth comes in judgment. The corruptible riches of the wealthy, now moth-eaten garments and rusting gold and silver, are revealed as stored wrath against them.[34] In addition to Will's debate with Scripture, the enigmatic scene in which Piers tears the pardon that promises good or evil to each according to his works[35] and the poem's theological speculation about the salvation of righteous heathens such as Trajan[36] exhibit the same tension concerning the neccesity of works for salvation.

Productive work and Christian works are inextricably linked in *Piers Plowman*, twin responsibilities for the Christian who hopes for salvation. Langland exhibits both traditional and contemporary attitudes toward work and works. After Hunger punishes those who will not work, he cites Genesis and Proverbs 20:4 to explain the nature of work to Piers:

> Go to Genesis þae geaunt, engendrour of vs alle;
> *In sudore* and swynk þow shalt þi mete tilie.
> And Sapience seiþ þe same--I seiȝ it in þe bible:
> *Piger propter frigus* no feeld wolde tilie;
> He shal go begge and bidde and no man bette his hunger.[37]

Hunger's Old Testament sources define work under the Old Law as a punishment and a condition for survival. Langland, however, also depicts the place of work under the New Law. Reflecting the growing moral importance of work in Christian society, Langland shows the Pentecost transforming work from a penalty for sin to a gift given by Grace herself. In the vision in Passus XIX in which the Holy Spirit comes down on Piers and his company, Grace distributes gifts to all people. These "graces" are not the usual virtues, however, but vocations: some men are suited to earn a living by speaking, such as lawyers and preachers; some are laborers; some are artisans; some buy and sell; some even steal back what false men have wrongfully taken.[38] Grace bestows every sort of vocation, regardless of *status*, and stresses the importance of mutual respect and cooperation among those of various vocations:

> And alle he lered to be lele, and ech a craft loue ooþer,
> Ne no boost ne debat be among hem alle.
> 'Thouȝ some be clenner þan some, ye se wel', quod Grace,
> That al craft and konnyng come of my ȝifte.
> Lokeþ þat noon lakke ooþer, but loueþ as breþeren;
> And who þat moost maistries kan be myldest of berynge.[39]

With work clearly defined as a God-given gift and responsibility, *Piers Plowman* advocates the return to traditional work as the means to Christian perfection, both individual and social, and rejects the consumerism of the growing market economy. This social regeneration, however, depends on individual moral reform in *Piers Plowman*; Christians who wish to imitate Christ must progress as Jesus did from *dowel* to *dobet* to *dobest*.[40] In Passus XIX Langland presents the Life of Christ as such a progression: Jesus "bigan god of his grace to do wel"[41] with his first miracle at the wedding at Cana; he began to *dobet* when he healed the sick, fed the multitudes, helped and healed all who asked, died and rose, and was called Son of David for "þe dedes þat he dide";[42] he began to *dobest* when he gave Peter the power to pardon. After his resurrection, Jesus appeared to Thomas and the frightened disciples in the upper room:

> And whan þis dede was doon do best he þouȝte
> And yaf Piers pardon, and power he grauntede hym,
> Myght men to assoille of all manere synnes,
> To all maner men mercy and forȝifnesse

In couenaunt þat þei come and kneweliche to paie
To Piers pardon þe Plowman *redde quod debes*.[43]

Those who *dobest* follow and administer the principle of justice and economy. When the Holy Spirit descends on Piers and his companions, he gives them the power to *dobest*—the power to perform works—and sends Grace to distribute the occupations that should ensure proper work. To become more perfect Christians, believers must act; they must elevate the number and sort of Christian works they perform;[44] they must imitate Christ by accepting and performing faithfully the work God gave them to do. Piers thus represents both individual and communal deliverance: he embodies both Christians' spiritual progress from *dowel* to *dobet* to *dobest* as well as the collective return to traditional work for the good of the community.[45] As the ideal Christian working for both his own salvation and the common good, Piers promises to provide for "alle kynne crafty men þat konne lyuen in truþe,"[46] but he also warns those who will not work as they should—*wastours*, fake beggars, prostitutes, jugglers, gamblers—that their souls are in peril:

Truþe tolde me ones and bad me telle if forþ:
Deleantur de libro viuencium; I sholde noȝt dele wiþ hem,
For holy chirche is holde of hem no tiþe to aske,
Quia cum iustis non scribantur.[47]

Christians who seek salvation must not only perform Christian works, but engage in productive work as well.

If Langland urges his fellow Christians both to perform Christian works and to engage in appropriate earthly occupations, he also urges them not to work too much, even for legitimate earthly profit, but only to work as much as they need in order to sustain simple lives. After Piers plows the half-acre and calls down Hunger to afflict Wastour in Passus VI, Truth sends Piers to till the earth again, but we next see Piers tearing the pardon and seemingly rejecting its message, that those who have done good works will go into life everlasting and those who have done evil into everlasting fire.[48] As Mary C. Schroeder (Carruthers) notes, Piers's tearing the pardon in a scenario similar to Moses breaking the tablets of the Ten Commandments may instead suggest a completion of that law.[49] Piers, the man who has already completed his work and satisfied the requirements of the Old Law, is now bound by its insufficiency to stop working and to care for his soul. From now on, Piers the Plowman will no longer merely provide for peoples' physical needs, but their spiritual needs as well; from now on, he will become one with Christ and the Church, just as Jesus takes on the person and arms of Piers and plows the fields with the Gospels in Passus XIX. The plowman no longer provides mere bread, but spiritual food; he gives not only of his produce, but himself; and he plows not with metal but with prayer, promising

> Of preieres and of penaunce my plouȝ shal ben herafter,
> And wepen whan I sholde werche þouȝ whete breed me faille.[50]

Underscoring the distinction between legitimate business and sinful busyness in the Middle Ages, Piers's decision to work less and to let God provide presents a model for ideal clerical poverty:

> The prophete his payn eet in penaunce and in sorwe
> By þat þe Sauter vs seith, and so did othere manye.
> That loueþ god lelly his liflode is ful esy;
> *Fuerunt michi lacrime mee panes die ac nocte.*
> And but if luc lye he lereþ vs anoþer
> By foweles þat are noȝt bisy about þe bely ioye;
> *Ne soliciti sitis* he seiþ in þe gospel,
> And sheweþ vs by ensample vs selue to wisse.
> The foweles in þe firmament, who fynt hem at wynter?
> Whan þe frost freseþ fode hem bihoueþ;
> Haue þei no gerner to go to but fod fynt hem alle.[51]

With an ideal strikingly similar to that of St. Francis, who rejected his father's thriving business for a life of voluntary poverty, Piers rejects the commercial aspirations of fourteenth-century clerics and argues with the priest who, noting that Piers is "lettred a litel," suggests to Piers that he could preach when he liked if he were a priest, thus calling to mind contemporary clerical abuses of the friars and other clerics who tried to profit from their offices.

Piers's assertion of clerical poverty here may explain the enigmatic pardon scene which precedes it if we carefully consider the role of the priest whom Piers opposes. Piers's anger as he tears the pardon is not in response to the letter of the pardon, but a reaction to the priest who rejects it and translates the Latin of the pardon, which "was writen riȝt þus in witnesse of truþe," as a threat rather than as an promise of justice:

> 'Peter!' quod þe preest þoo, 'I kan no pardon fynde
> But do wel and haue wel, and god shal haue þi soule,
> And do yuel and haue yuel, and hope þow noon ooþer
> That after þi deeþ day þe deuel shal haue þi soule.'[52]

Key to understanding why the priest *gloses* his passage and why Piers grows angry, the passage that immediately precedes the priest's request to see and translate the pardon describes precisely those who are not able to work as exempt from such responsibilities:

> Ac elde men and hore þat helplees ben of strengþe,
> And wommen wiþ child þat werche ne mowe,
> Blynde and bedreden and broken hire membres
> That taken þis myschief mekeliche as Mesels and oþere,
> Han as pleyn pardon as þe Plowman hymselue;
> For loue of hir lowe herte oure lord haþ hem graunted
> Hit penaunce and hir Purgatorie vpon þis pure erþe.[53]

Exempt from the responsibility of work just as plainly as Piers has satisfied the requirement, the poor have their penitential debt already paid by Christ. The priest, however, emphasizes not reward, but punishment in his translation. Rejecting the pardon as an assurance of justice, the priest denies the poor their pardon and exemption and instead stresses punishment, implying that they need greater penance and good works if they wish to avoid Purgatory. A clear excuse to sell indulgences, the priest's interpretation of the pardon suggests he is one who will take from the poor when he should give, a practice the priest advocates when he suggests that Piers take up a life of preaching. What angers Piers is probably not the pardon, but the priest's perversion of justice and willingness to use the text for monetary gain at the expense of the poor, who are already exempt; instead of living a life of voluntary poverty as Piers plans, clerics twist their texts to take advantage of the poor for personal gain. And by using such texts to sell indulgences, preachers distort the necessity of Christian works and an honest living into a calls for monetary payments. Instead of doing their proper work and helping the poor, such clerics further harm them and thus undermine Christ's Church.

Returning to the question of whether work is necessary at all for salvation and, if it is, to what degree, we can probably agree that *Piers Plowman* asserts the necessity of works for those who are physically able at the same time as it suggests ethical boundaries for that work. But just how much work is enough before one's debt is paid, however, depends on what one is given to do, and sometimes the willingness to work is more important than the quantity of work or works done. One's intentions thus become significant in determining whether one earns one's reward or not, regardless of just how much work one is able or asked to perform. The scriptural basis for this idea, Jesus' parable of the vineyard workers hired at different parts of the day and paid the same suggests that while all will receive at least the promised reward by performing the promised work, which is the essence of Piers's pardon and Old Testament justice, under the New Law God rewards equally those workers called both early and late, regardless of how late the householder calls them to work. Agreeing to work and then working faithfully when God asks is clearly all that is required for Christians to be eligible to receive the promised reward, the salvation Christ offers. In addition to rewarding equally all faithful workers, early or late, the householder makes those who have been in the field the longest wait for their pay until he rewards latecomers, about which those who worked all day in the heat complain. Rebuking a complainer, the lord replies:

> Friend, I do thee no wrong: didst thou not agree to with me for a penny? Take what is thine, and go thy way: I will also give to this last even as to thee. Or, is it not lawful for me to do what I will? Is thy eye evil, because I am good? So shall the last be first, and the first last. For many are called, but few chosen.[54]

The generosity of God, the sacrifice of Jesus and the gift of eternal life, offers the gift of salvation to all faithful Christians who work as they are called, regardless of when that moment is. The parable not only evokes the spirit of the New Law, but suggests that some workers in the vineyard are called to harder and longer work than others, an idea Langland supports as well when he points out the greater responsibilities of the clergy, those whom God chooses for early and long work in his vineyard through their vocational calling.

Langland's traditional Christian attitude towards works, sacrifice, and the redemption of sins favors personal and physical sacrifice over the sacrifice of wealth. In the Letter to the Hebrews, Paul describes how sacrifices under the Old Law were inferior to the ultimate and personal sacrifice of Jesus:

> But Christ, being come an high priest of the good things to come, by a greater and more perfect tabernacle not made with hand, that is, not of this creation: Neither by the blood of goats, or of calves, but by his own blood, entered once into the holies,

> having obtained eternal redemption. For if the blood of goats and of oxen, and the ashes of an heifer being sprinkled, sanctify such as are defiled, to the cleansing of the flesh: How much more shall the blood of Christ, who by the Holy Ghost offered himself unspotted unto God, cleanse our conscience from dead works, to serve the living God.[55]

This passage emphasizes the difference between Jesus' sacrifice of self and the sacrifice of wealth enacted in offering sacrifices of agricultural and husbandry. The unique and personal sacrifice of Jesus requires that those who wish to follow Jesus must also make sacrifices of a unique and personal nature. Rejecting the sacrifice of the products of human labor and focusing instead on works of self-sacrifice, Paul's allegorical reading of Old Testament sacrifice urges Christians who wish to imitate Christ to eschew "dead works," here the sacrificial animals.

Peter also marks the inferiority of sacrificing wealth not only in the form of animals, but in the form of money when he compares Jesus' sacrifice to corruptible sacrifices:

> Knowing that you were not redeemed with corruptible things as gold or silver, from your vain conversation of the tradition of your fathers: But with the precious blood of Christ, as of a lamb unspotted and undefiled, Foreknown indeed before the foundation of the world, but manifested in the last times for you.[56]

Here we again see the distinction between primary and secondary sacrifice, between sacrifice of the self and sacrifice of what is external to oneself, the product of one's labor. Substituting corruptible goods for self sacrifice is no way for a Christian to imitate Christ, for a secondary sacrifice cannot replace first-hand Christian works. Making a monetary donation to a confessor is a tertiary sacrifice another step removed from secondary sacrifice; less immediate than the material product of work, money only represents the value of material goods. The least acceptable type of sacrifice, a payment of money is worth even less than a material sacrifice.[57]

Parallel to the distinction between primary, secondary, and tertiary sacrifice is the growing distinction in the later Middle Ages between primary, secondary, and tertiary occupations. While primary sacrifice, primary occupations, and most secondary occupations involve personal physical work(s), tertiary sacrifices and tertiary are less physical and are marked by the manipulation of wealth, the product of work, rather than actual work(s). Those in primary occupations, such as field laborers, are directly productive; those in secondary occupations, such as bakers, make products out of other products; and those in tertiary occupations, including lawyers, teachers, prostitutes, bankers, merchants, and entertainers, make no products at all, almost always work for money, and usually dwell in urban areas.[58]

Many members of tertiary occupations did not fit into the traditional vocations of praying, fighting, and laboring, and for orthodox reformists like Langland, such non-productive toil for cash was morally suspect and inferior to primary work(s). Langland's anxiety about his own work as a poet, a tertiary occupation, is apparent in his distinction between one of *goddes gleman* and a minstrel like the taverngoer who embodies Sloth.[59]

Restrictions on who could perform primary work also suggest the growing moral and salvific power conferred on work in the later Middle Ages. For example, Le Goff points out that as the period proceeded, Jews were barred from most primary and secondary occupations and left to engage in tertiary occupations such as usury and medicine.[60] A large part of the moral disapproval of such work stems from the belief that the "goods" that those in tertiary occupations "sold"—legal advice, knowledge, their own time—was not theirs to sell.[61] If those in tertiary occupations sold that which was not theirs to sell, all the money they earned was ill-gotten. Like usurers, who sinned against God and nature by making money multiply as if it were living,[62] others in tertiary occupations could easily be criticized for making money unnaturally—that is, without doing proper, productive work.[63]

Tertiary occupations thus challenged customary economic practices for setting price levels, for a "just price" in the Middle Ages was a going market rate based on the value of the goods being sold plus expenses, such as transportation, and maintenance, which represented the money one needed to support one's family. Those in tertiary occupations had no goods to assess, which made any fee suspect. With no goods to set a base value on professional fees, such fees were free to soar, leaving services such as legal assistance going to the highest bidder and thus undermining justice. Le Goff notes that growing concerns about economic justice parallel the growth in the market economy:

> [The] preoccupation with *justice* became a dominant idea in the economic domain, which was so steeped in religious ideology and ethics. The *just price* and the *just wage* were the fundamental themes for economic activity, and for the marketplace then beginning to take shape. Even though the "just" price was, to be accurate, merely the market price, demand for justice was present.[64]

The growing "demand for justice" in economic life could indicate that such justice was becoming more and more difficult to obtain in the present system; it could also, however, indicate a growing belief that wronged members of society could demand justice and retribution, an idea no doubt familiar to the rebels of 1381.

The economic concept of the "just price" in the social sphere complemented the religious concept of satisfaction for individuals' sins; just as the Church expected merchants to sell goods at a "just price," it expected sinners to pay a "just price"—reparation plus penalty—for their transgressions. Because just how much one "owed" depended not only on what one's sins were, but what one's social obligations were, Langland suggests that members of the clergy are more likely to fall short in meeting their obligations than laborers are, for clerics have a greater charge:

> I se ensamples myself and so may manye oþere,
> That seruauntȝ þat seruen lordes selde fallen in arerage,
> But þo þat kepen þe lordes catel, clerkes and Reues.
> Right so lewed laborers and of litel knowyng
> Selden falle so foule and so fer in synne
> As clerkes of holy kirke þat kepen cristes tresor,
> The which is mannes soule to saue, as god seiþ in þe gospel:
> *Ite vos in vineam meam.*[65]

Langland here asserts that the clergy, who should concern themselves with saving God's treasure, the souls of Christians, instead focus on obtaining treasure from their benefactors. Reflecting on the difference between true and false treasure, Langland echoes the Bibilical distinction between earthly and heavenly, material and spiritual riches.[66] Holy Church also differentiates between treasures true and false, spiritual and material, when she distinguishes between Truth, the best treasure,[67] and the treasure which the inhabitant of the "dongeon in þe dale,"[68] the "castel of care,"[69] offers:

> TherInne wonyeþ a wye þat wrong is yhote;
> Fader of falshede, he founded it hymselue.
> Adam and Eue he egged to ille,
> Counseilled Kaym to killen his broþer,
> Iudas he iaped wiþ iewen siluer

> And siþen on an Eller hanged hym after.
> He is lettere of loue, lieþ hem alle;
> That trusten on his tresour bitrayed are sonnest.[70]

At first glance, Holy Church's figure of treasure appears to be just another case of a materialist metaphor creeping into a religious debate, but where one lays up one's treasures in the New Testament—either on earth or in heaven—indicates whether one is worldly and doomed or holy and redeemed.[71] Holy Church's mention of treasure also points to a distinction between treasure and money, to a clash between the values of a gift economy and the realities of a profit economy. Little sums up the tension: "The received tradition was in fact biased against all the main elements of the new economy: against cities, against money, and against the urban professions."[72] Langland's labelling money and the material goods it can buy "false treasure" not only distinguishes between spiritual and material wealth, but between traditional feudal values and the market economy.[73]

In a feudal society, treasure is a gift, a sign of allegiance and loyalty, and both the act of giving and continued presence of the object binds community members by reminding them of their social and political obligations.[74] "True" treasure inspires *trouth*, the binding tie of feudal organization. Moreover, for the Church, treasures such as gold vessels are fitting adornments, signs of sacrifice of wealth to the glory of God.

Money, on the other hand, is interchangeable, anonymous, and durable.[75] Its presence inspires no memory of the giver, and it has no history or value as a political relic, as the sword of a slain ruler has. In his work on the origin of money, André Orléan affirms that money "as a means of storing value, as a source of arbitrary power in relation to the rest of society, and as breaking the infinite chain of reciprocal bonds, is a threat to the holistic order,"[76] which we can define in the Middle Ages as the feudal and religious bonds enacted in the exchange or gift of treasure.[77] Money, on the other hand, inspires little loyalty beyond that which is commercially profitable and thus puts most allegiances up for sale. Little describes the outlook on money that developed during the shift from a gift to a moneyed economy:

> Attitudes towards money did not shift abruptly from one of awe before precious treasure to one of habital acceptance of it as a practical, everyday tool. In something of an intervening stage, money was seen as an instrument of exchange that had devil-

> like, magical powers of luring people and then of corrupting them. The traditional theological programme of the virtues and vices invested in avarice some of these same powers.[78]

Medieval Christians who warned of the dangers of money and condemned the accumulation of wealth had tradition on their side. New Testament examples of the moral danger of money and wealth abound, from Jesus' assertion that it is easier for a camel to pass through the eye of a needle than for a rich man to enter heaven,[79] to Judas's blood money to the sudden deaths of Ananias and Saphira for withholding some money from Peter and the disciples from the sale of a piece of land.[80] In his commentary on Matt. 6:24, Augustine warns that whoever seeks riches and his own profit serves the "prince of this world."[81] Langland displays his knowledge of such traditional sentiments:

> Kynghod and knyȝthod, for auȝt I kan awayte,
> Helpeþ noȝt to heuenward at oone yeris ende,
> Ne richesse ne rentes ne Reauee of lordes.
> Poule preueþ it impossible, riche men in heuene:
> Salomon seiþ also þat siluer is worst to louye:
> *Nichil iniquius quam amare pecuniam*;
> And Caton kenneþ vs to wilne no richesse,
> And preiseden pouerte with pacience; þe Apostles bereþ witnesse
> That þei han Eritage in heuene, and by trewe riȝt,
> Ther riche men no riȝt may cleyme but of ruþe and grace.[82]

Reacting to the clash between the growing material wealth of the Church and Christian praise of poverty, Langland condemns the Church's accumulation of wealth and urges institutional economic reform including returning land to disenfranchised heirs and opening Constantine's coffers.[83] Describing how a king will come to correct the religious who do not keep their rule, Langland warns of an impending apocalyptic battle:

> Ac er þat kyng come Caym shal awake,
> Ac dowel shal dyngen hym adoun and destruye his myȝte.[84]

The millennial rule of *þat king* follows the battle against the fellowship of Antichrist, which includes Cain, who rises from the dead for the battle. Cain, the first husbandman, could be described not only as a follower of Antichrist, but as anti-Piers. While Piers works for the common good, Cain worked for his own aggrandizement; while Piers feeds the hungry to save their lives, Cain killed his brother, a shepherd like Christ. In Langland's apocalyptic narrative, Cain returns and battles Piers and his company; the true plowman overcomes the false and Christ returns as husbandman to gather the souls grown ripe for harvest, the fruit of Piers.

The clergy's charge to tend the Lord's vineyard, to nurture the fruit of Piers, is just one of many pastoral and rural metaphors that describe the proper work of Christians and their pastors.[85] Just as the quality and quantity of rural labor, barring drought or other calamity, can be measured by the harvest, the efforts of the clergy will be measured by the human harvest of saved souls they cultivate. Reflecting both the agricultural imagery of the Bible and the real crisis in rural life in the late fourteenth century, Langland's apocalyptic expression is rural in character, for the agricultural images, allegories, and metaphors in the poem—most notably the plowman, the tree of charity, and the fruit of Piers—link rural production and salvation.

The agricultural imagery of *Piers Plowman* is extensive, as is the store of biblical and apocalyptic agricultural metaphor. While the subject is too vast to address here fully, we can discern the relationship between agricultural work and the Day of Judgment by examining the relationship between plowing and the harvest. Bloomfield summarizes the tradition:

> The harvest is paradise or salvation, and those who tend it lead man to his proper end. Christ is the supreme harvester or plowman, and all plowmen to some extent are symbols of his true followers—priests, religious, or even laymen who are creating or bringing in the harvest. Jesus was historically a carpenter and could be associated with the making of plows. The plow is the tool whereby He prepares the field of the world for His harvest of souls. Just as Pentecost is the feast of the Church, of the mission, of the Holy Ghost, and also the feast of the end of time, of the Church Triumphant, so the Plowman is both the ecclesiastical and eschatological image par excellence.[86]

The figure of Piers thus links poverty, hard work and salvation. While Stephen A. Barney explores the figure of Piers and its "cultural antecedents"[87] to demonstrate that Langland's plowman represents a priest and preacher, we should note that Piers appears at various times as members of all three estates: he is a plowman, a priest, and a knight. The ideal Christian performing work appropriate to his *status*, Piers represents all good, working Christians, but for fourteenth-century Christians, he was particularly resonant as a representative of the rural poor, as Bloomfield notes.[88]

Throughout *Piers Plowman*, we find not only extensive representations of agricultural life, but a preoccupation with the products of economic life, such as food and clothing. Bloomfield calls our attention to the relationship between the apocalyptic elements of *Piers Plowman* and its images of food, clothing, and agricultural, claiming "the basic symbol of the poem, Piers, and its attendant agricultural imagery, together with other important classes of images in the poem, such as food and clothing, reinforce the apocalyptic point."[89] Although Bloomfield interprets the recurring images of food and clothing as "grace and perfection symbols,"[90] we should note that while food and clothing sometimes suggest grace or perfection, they can just as easily suggest disaster. Although the bread of the Eucharist imparts grace, food is dangerous from the first bite of Eden's apple to the excess and *wanhope* of Gluttony. And although Christ's donning the armor of Piers signifies Jesus' incarnation, his accepting human nature to redeem it,[91] the rich array of Meed and Hawkin's coat of sins should make us cautious about associating clothing with grace. More likely than their appearing as symbols of perfection, images of food and clothing recur in *Piers Plowman* because, like Meed, they are necessary for living and morally neutral until they are used or abused and because their contemporary abuses were central to Langland's assertions that moral reform was imminent and necessary.

According to Robertson and Huppé, the images of food and clothing in *Piers* help unify the poem, and Bloomfield notes that for Langland, the "active basis of justice in society is the doctrine of superfluity and, as Robertson and Huppé say, its necessary measuring rod, need."[92] Like money, food and clothing are not sinful when properly used, but only when used beyond measure. Use beyond measure implies a gross imbalance in means, general superfluity, or both, and is characteristic of a moneyed economy, which offers the rich the ability to store wealth conveniently. In Langland's time, the concentration of wealth and the conspicuous consumption it drove[93] marked the growth of the sort of "needs" we who live in a commercial culture are all too familiar with—those created by the very possibility of consumption and by comparing our own belongings with the possessions of others. Robert Adams, however, notes that Need is not uncompromisingly positive or negative in Piers, for Langland both vilifies avaricious consumers and praises the patient poor: "Need, though never neutral in effect, is a personification of an ethically neutral condition. The morality or wisdom of his advice is only definable in terms of the other characters with whom he interacts."[94] Like Meed, Need's morality depends on the company he keeps. Just as Conscience explains to the king that there are two types of Meed, good and bad, and characterizes bad Meed as *Mede mesureless,*[95] Need can be either good or bad, depending on whether need is real or created by avarice and the desires of a developing consumer culture.

In Passus I, Langland asserts that people truly need only three things: clothing, food and drink. Echoing Church Fathers such as Ambrose and scholars such as Thomas Aquinas,[96] Holy Church reminds the dreamer that Truth, the father of faith, the creator of all, commanded that the earth provide for all people:

> Of wollene, of lynnen, of liflode at nede
> In mesurable manere to make yow at ese;
> And comaunded of his curteisie in commune þree þynges;
> Are none nedfulle but þo; and nempne hem I þynke
> And rekene hem by reson: reherce þow after.
> That oon is vesture from chele þee to saue;
> That oþer is mete at meel for mysese of þiselue;
> And drynke whan þee drieþ, ac do it noȝt out of reson
> That þow worþe þe wers whan þow werche sholdest.[97]

People only need enough clothing to keep from being cold, enough food to stave off hunger, and enough drink to quench thirst; consumption or possession beyond what is "ynogh"[98] is out of measure, "out of reson." In *Piers Plowman*, these sorts of needs, false needs, are described as a product of Antichrist's work:

> Whan nede hadde vndernome me þus anoon I fil aslepe
> And mette ful merueillously þat in mannes forme
> Antecrist cam þanne, and all crop of truþe
> Torned it tid vp so doun and ouertilte þe roote,
> And made fals sprunge and sprede and spede mennes nedes.[99]

Robert Adams notes that Antichrist closely follows Need in the apocalyptic drama near the end of the poem and asserts that in this episode "Langland is not only dramatizing an apocalyptic scriptural text but also a specific commentary tradition on that text," a tradition that represented Need as growing worldliness in the final days.[100] Need going before the Antichrist leads Adams to conclude that Langland believed he was living in the final days:

> Langland seems to have believed that he was seeing the end of the world in his lifetime. All the evidence surrounding the parable of Need indicates that he is depicting nothing less than the tribulation under the last great Antichrist and that he thinks these events have already begun or will begin shortly.[101]

Adams supports his argument that Langland expects the final Antichrist by noting that the poet does not make use of the tradition based on 1 John 2:18, which "envisioned numerous antichrists as precursors to the last and most terrible"[102] and by calling our attention to Will's last dream, in which Antichrist comes *in mannes forme*: "Such an explicit avowal seems designed to underscore the very point so commonly denied today, that no vague social forces, no mere bad men, indeed nothing less than the great 'son of perdition' himself is here intended."[103] Although I agree with Adams that Need is an important precursor to the apocalyptic visions at the end of *Piers Plowman*, I do not believe that Langland ever expected a single Antichrist—*the* Antichrist—to appear in his lifetime. Langland would no more expect to encounter an individual who is the final Antichrist than to meet the "real" Piers. Like Piers, Antichrist shifts shapes; just as Piers appears as a plowman, Simon Peter, Christ the Knight, and the Good Samaritan, Antichrist appears as an avaricious friar, a deceptive doctor, and a rural vagrant who destroys fields. While Adams is correct to note that Langland's Antichrist is not a "vague social force" or just "bad men," his argument that Langland expects "the" Antichrist to materialize is undermined by the poem's multiple representations of Antichrist and Langland's shifting allegory. When Langland's Antichrist comes *in mannes forme*, he comes as many different men, working through his company just as Christ works through Piers and the church. Along the same lines, Langland's utopian passages describing the coming of a king to restore order, justice, and peace do not necessarily announce the return of Christ himself, but could anticipate the ascendence of an English king to reform English society and fulfill the responsibilities of a true Christian ruler.

In addition to the scriptural tradition Adams explores, we should also note that Need has an historical correlative—the famine early in the fourteenth century, a time of real need personified by Hunger, whom Piers calls to punish those who will not work in Passus VI. And as anyone familiar with a relative who lived through the Great Depression has probably witnessed first-hand, food shortages can later prompt the sort of wasteful activities that Langland identifies with the work of Antichrist, including both hoarding and conspicuous consumption. Whether Langland himself remembered the famine early in the fourteenth century or whether he had heard about it from the generation before him, the poet saw Need precede the works of Antichrist in his own century, sharpening his apocalyptic vision by offering an historical incidence of the scriptural verses Adams explores.

That Langland did not necessarily expect the final Antichrist to arrive does not mean that *Piers Plowman* is not an apocalyptic poem, but that Langland's apocalyptism leaned toward the tradition of regeneration, the tradition imbued with the rural imagery he used so freely. In the Augustinian tradition, Langland's eschatology is interiorized; the immediate end awaits the individual soul rather than society as a whole, expressed by Langland in the salvific trajectory of the individual from *dowel* to *dobet* to *dobest*. While Langland's poem surely exhibits apocalyptic fervor, Langland's constant calls for moral reform and his utopian passages point to a renewal of society, not to the end of time. While Adams concludes that the poet was convinced he was living in the last stage of the last age, I am more inclined to agree with Kerby-Fulton that Langland's "odd combination of grim pessimism and tenacious optimism, reactionary indignation and unflagging hope for large-scale renewal"[104] more closely resembles a sort of "reformist apocalypticism," a tradition more concerned with living in the last age than in ending it. *Piers Plowman*, after all, ends not with destruction or judgment, but with a pilgrimage to find Piers, the same pilgrimage repeated throughout the poem from its beginning. After Conscience faces Antichrist, he heads out again to find Piers, to find a way to live and work as a true Christian. Still, neither Langland nor his double, Will, works for reform himself, but instead roams the countryside, writes poetry, and begs money for praying for the dead. As much a product of the vocational upheaval of his time as those he depicts in his poem, Langland does not expect gradual economic reform, but authoritative intervention in the person of a just king.[105] Whether Langland awaits an English king or Christ the King, such an intervention does not promise steady institutional reform, but radical apocalyptic intervention—a renovation by fiat.

CHAPTER THREE

Demographics and Discontent in Fourteenth-Century England

One sign of the literary impact of the growing market economy and the widening gap between rich and poor in fourteenth-century England is the rise of venality satire in English. John A. Yunck points out that while attacks on wealth, especially ones directed at those in tertiary occupations such as lawyers, are fairly common in medieval Latin and French, virtually no venality satire appears in English before 1350.[1] In the second half of the fourteenth century, however, the theme of venality "appears almost everywhere."[2] The sudden crop of English venality satire suggests that monetary wealth grew as a disruptive force in the second half of the fourteenth century, a delay due in part to England's previously limited participation in the growing international market economy. The shifts in fourteenth-century English economic life that are the subject of this chapter—including changes in demographics, trade balance, currency valuation, and the relative purchasing power of various sectors of the economy—challenged traditional ethical norms and disrupted centuries-old patterns of social organization. The rise of venality satire in English in this period reflects the growing tension between traditional feudal Christian values and the realities of a growing market economy, a widening gap to which Langland reacts throughout *Piers Plowman*.

Sketching a picture of the shifting conditions of economic life in fourteenth-century England useful for literary scholars of the period is difficult, not only because economic discourse was inseparable from religious discourse in the Middle Ages, but because the array of historical evidence is susceptible to contradictory analysis. Harry A. Miskimin concedes that "our knowledge of the economic history of the later Middle Ages has not yet reached a classical state marked by universal accord among specialists."[3] Although economists and historians have considerable raw data from a variety of sources including mint records, wills, and tax rolls among others, such varied sources frustrate attempts to synthesize the data into a comprehensive and reliable representation of economic life in fourteenth-century England.[4]

Most economic historians who tackle this problem such as M. M. Postan and N. J. Mayhew would probably agree with Miskimin that "it is possible to produce quite different descriptions of the general price trend simply by varying the weights allotted to the components of the market basket or index" because "the prices of various classes of commodities exhibited divergent trends in the last half of the fourteenth century."[5] As a result, economic historians "can conceive of two individuals with different consumption habits" who undergo "entirely opposite effects from the price movements, one suffering an erosion, the other enjoying an appreciation, of the purchasing power of his income."[6] Partial descriptions of the medieval English economy thus yield various conclusions depending on which part of the elephant the economic historian grasps.

Experts still debate not only the effects but the causes of economic contraction in the second half of the fourteenth century. Economic historians dispute the relative importance and timing of such factors as demographic change, bullion availability, and shifting trade balances in precipitating the economic crises of the century. Even without consensus on these issues, those of us who are interested in the social and literary products of the times are lucky to have ample evidence to consider how factors such as famine and plague, money shortages, and shifts in production and consumption contributed to the overall awareness of crisis and change that Langland and a number of his contemporaries exhibit.

The demographic changes of the fourteenth century began with changes in the environment that reduced agricultural production. Early in the century, a warm spell that Europe experienced for almost half a millennium gave way to a period of wet, cold weather.[7] England had experienced considerable population growth during the warmer period; the Domesday survey of 1086 records a population of 1.1 million, which J. C. Russell estimates rose to 3.75 million by the middle fourteenth century.[8] This figure would have been slightly higher were it not for the famine earlier in the century, for the rains and colder weather of the early century reduced agricultural production in England and throughout much of northern Europe.

When Hunger appears in *Piers Plowman*, he attacks *wastours* in the countryside who will not do the agricultural work that Piers asks of them. Frightened, some fakers flee into barns to flail themselves; for a humble pot of peas from Piers, hermits cut their copes into short coats and "wente as werkmen to wedynge and mowynge / And doluen drit and dung to ditte out hunger."[9] The abnormally great rainfall of 1314 initiated the first of the century's food shortages. Helen Robbins lists famine periods for England as 1315–16, 1351, and 1369, with a "semi-famine" in 1321, and Miskimin describes 1315–17 as the period of the "Great European famine."[10] We know that Langland witnessed another such shortage in 1370, for in Passus XIII of *Piers Plowman*, Hawkin the active man describes this food shortage in London:

> There was a careful commune whan no cart com to towne
> Wiþ bake breed fro Stratford; þo gonnen beggeris wepe
> And werkmen were agast a lite; þis wole be þouȝte longe:
> In þe date of oure driȝte, in a drye Aprill,
> A thousand and þre hundred, twies þritty and ten,
> My wafres were gesene whan Chichestre was Maire.[11]

One would expect food shortages to be worse in towns than in the country because of the towns' greater population density, but food shortages actually made city and town life more attractive, for trade alliances and the wealth of urban inhabitants provided a buffer against starvation. Miskimin points out that London had a relatively low mortality rate in the great famine, while "the death rate marched upward parallel with the price of grain" in the countryside, for "private urban stocks and foreign imports had rendered London's upper classes virtually immune from famine in a time when the farmers themselves suffered and died of starvation."[12] Whether we consider the Great Famine earlier in the century or the smaller famines after the plague, food shortages hit the countryside at least as hard as larger urban areas.

In addition to weakening the population, famine fostered internal migration, which hastened the spread of the plague by "break[ing] down the relative isolation of the smaller village and agricultural communities" and "reducing the effectiveness of the natural quarantine imposed by village life in the Middle Ages."[13] As people like Langland's dreamer roamed in search of food, they helped spread the plague throughout the countryside and to the towns.

Overestimating the demographic impact of the plague is difficult. By killing about a third of the population, the plague simultaneously caused a scarcity of labor and a sharp decline in the demand for food. By reducing both the labor supply and the domestic demand for grain, the plague hastened the growth of the towns and weakened what was left of the manorial system in England, for the plague made it feasible to abandon the system most efficient for producing the large quantities of food that a growing population demanded. The impact of the plague on England's agricultural economy was serious, for as Miskimin notes, "rents fell, acreage was allowed to revert to forest or waste, wages rose reflecting the enhanced economic value of the worker, and the profits of the agricultural sector were diminished" as a result of the plague's effect on the population.[14] Steady prices in a shrunken market diminished agricultural profits, but because both the demand for grain and the production of grain decreased simultaneously, the prices of agricultural products after the plague remained surprisingly consistent with pre-plague price levels. Stagnant prices exacerbated the economic effects the agricultural sector already felt from the sharp decrease in demand for goods.

Price indices from the second half of the fourteenth century suggest an important trend: the increasing flow of money in the towns. At the same time that the agricultural base of the economy contracted, the sectors of the economy based in the towns steadily increased wages, prices and profits. The relative price levels for various economic activities after the plague show the decline of agriculture in England relative to other economic activities. [15] As the prices of items such as horseshoes and ploughshares escalated along with the cost of labor, agricultural production costs increased significantly. Higher prices for metal farm implements also indicate a greater demand for such materials, quite possibly for armaments in the war with France. As it was economically advantageous for rural workers to sell any excess equipment for the metal market, and because the plague left idle equipment, we should not be surprised to see ploughshares beaten into weapons in a direct reversal of the biblical injunction that Langland reminds his readers of in Passus III.[16] In *Piers Plowman*, when Reason reigns over true Christian society

> Alle þat beren baselard, brood swerd or launce,
> Ax ouþer hachet or any wepene ellis,
> Shal be demed to þe deeþ but if he do it smyþye
> Into sikel or to siþe, to Shaar or to kultour:
> *Conflabunt gladios suos in vomeres &c.*
> Ech man to pleye with a plow, Pyckoise or spade,
> Spynne or sprede donge or spille hymself with sleuþe.[17]

This millenarian vision reverses the contemporary trend and perhaps even reflects Langland's knowledge of those participating in the 1381 Uprising who used their agricultural implements as weapons.[18]

John Gower also stresses the link between war and riches, between violence and the perversion of a properly agricultural society devoted to working for the common good into one committed to making and protecting profits. At the beginning of Book V of the *Confessio Amantis*, the book about Avarice, Gower explains that when God first made the world, all was held in common, but once "men knewen the moneie"

> Tho wente pes out of the weie
> And werre cam on every side,
> Which alle love leide aside
> and of comun his propre made,
> So that in stede of schovele and spade
> The scharpe swerd was take on honde;
> And in thise wise it cam to londe,
> Whereof men maden dyches depe
> And hyhe walles forto kepe
> The gold which Avarice encloseth.[19]

Both Gower and Langland set agricultural work in opposition to the work of war by setting agricultural implements in opposition to weapons. Neither poet misses the opportunity to criticize wartime expenditures that come at the expense of the people of the countryside.

While producers of basic manufactured goods enjoyed inflated prices, agricultural producers endured steady prices at the same time that their material and labor costs rose. By the second half of the fourteenth century, the contraction in agriculture relative to the expansion of trade and basic manufacturing such as we see in the wool trade put grain producers at a comparative disadvantage. As a result, money steadily flowed from agricultural regions to the towns, as Miskimin explains:

> Towns paid less for goods and sold their own products for more; as a result, money tended to accumulate in urban centers. Increased taxation and the migration of wealthy landlords to the more secure cities accelerated the outflow of rural funds and

> compounded the already observable pressures tending to demonetize the countryside by forcibly removing funds in the form of rents and taxes. When this began to happen, the rural portion of urban prosperity which had been based upon the divergence between the prices of manufactured and of agricultural products could last only so long as it took to drain the countryside of funds.[20]

In Langland's time, rural areas were already short on money. Miskimin points out that the countryside ran out of money by the beginning of the fifteenth century, thereby helping to force down the prices of manufactured goods and to restore the balance between the agricultural and manufacturing sectors of the economy.[21]

Changes in tax assessment also helped drain money from rural areas. Before 1334, the lay subsidy was based on local assessments of peasants' movable goods. The method of assessment changed in 1334 when the government nominated commissioners "to negotiate a collective agreement within each village community . . . . The government was guaranteed a fixed return, which remained the same for about a century in spite of the drastic population fall after 1349."[22] With pre-plague negotiations still in force, payments "could seriously deplete the cash reserves of even relatively prosperous tenants whose assets were more likely to be in grain, livestock and equipment than in money."[23]

In yet another way the plague contributed to the shift of wealth to the towns by concentrating it in the hands of fewer individuals. In the towns, people had more money not only because of higher wages and better prices for their goods, but because these "free funds" were "supplemented through the concentration of wealth as a result of the inheritance effects of the plagues" as survivors, "stimulated by sudden affluence and fear of death . . . spent freely either on luxury or salvation."[24] As surviving relatives accrued the bequests of their decimated families, those individuals whose families already had money often enjoyed the concentrated wealth of several of their deceased relatives, a trend supported by the number of wills probated in London in the fifties and sixties.[25] The Church also clearly benefitted from this concentration of wealth, for those who had no remaining heirs often left their entire estates to the Church in the hopes of salvation, and others made donations in hopes of survival during plague time[26] and for the souls of departed relatives. With greater resources and an awareness of how fleeting earthly life can be, many survivors increased their per capita spending significantly. Those who sought luxury in the form of exotic goods and salvation in the administration of sacraments would most readily find such products and services in the towns.

Big spenders in town did not, however, provide growing markets for those in the agricultural sector. Regardless of one's resources, one can only consume a finite amount of food, and perishable agricultural products are not suited for accumulation. Miskimin points out that "it is a general rule that the portion of income expended for food varies inversely with income—the larger the income, the smaller the relative amount spent for food."[27] Increases in spending for food, moreover, were most likely to benefit merchants and foreign producers, who supplied more expensive victuals such as wine, than to benefit the rural grain market. In a time of conspicuous consumption, a few extra bottles of French wine were more impressive than storehouses of surplus peas. Instead of spending more on basics, buyers improved the quality of their diets; after the plague, people ate richer food and drank more wine. We can detect the increased demand for luxury foodstuffs by examining price indices for exotic foods. Miskimin compares the years 1261–1350 with the years 1351–1400 and notes that " the price index of foreign goods consisting of herring, wine, pepper, oil, sugar, almonds, and saffron rises to 162 against 100 in the earlier base period" while "[t]he indices for the two most important and heavily consumed commodities, herring and wine, rise respectively to 202 and 206."[28] Meat consumption also seems to have risen significantly in the second half of the fourteenth century, probably beginning with "something of a short-term glut on the London meat market in the years immediately following the Black Death, as landlords attempted to convert animals received as death taxes of entry fines into cash."[29] Meat production would also tend to increase because less land was under cultivation and was thus available for grazing and because feed prices remained relatively low.

Agricultural producers responded to the stagnant grain market by growing more crops for secondary consumption and for use in animal husbandry. Barley grew in importance as the period saw an increase in brewing, and grains used as fodder such as oats, peas, and other legumes "benefited from the demand derived from their use as secondary goods in stock raising."[30] Although they were not aware of our modern concept of the market, late medieval suppliers certainly responded to changes in demand for their products.

Just as the newly rich turned to luxury foodstuffs, they developed a taste for luxury apparel. In the General Prologue to the *Canterbury Tales*, Chaucer's guildsmen and their wives, with their travelling cook and extravagant dress, portray accurately this sort of consumption pattern. The guildsmen are not content to earn or carry silver, but must ostentatiously display it as well:

> Ful fressh and newe hir geere apiked was;
> Hir knyves were chaped noght with bras
> But al with silver, wroght ful clene and weel,
> Hire girdles and hir pouches everydeel.[31]

For another portrait of conspicuous wealth, we need look no further than the industrious Wife of Bath in her extravagant coverchiefs, striking scarlet hose, huge hat and spurs.[32]

From the middle of the fourteenth century, discriminating consumers such as the guildmen and Wife demanded luxurious materials such as silk.[33] As more townspeople with discretionary funds spent excess wealth on apparel, whose manufacture constituted the primitive industrial base, they often violated social norms governing dress. Chaucer's Parson speaks at length about elaborate dress and food, which he considers two manifestations of the deadly sin of pride. His descriptions chronicle the extravagant fashions of the day:

> As to the first synne, that is in superfluitee of clothynge, which that maketh it so deeere, to harm of the peple; not oonly the cost of embrowdynge, the degise endentynge or barrynge, owndynge, palynge, wyndynge or bendyngeand semblable wast of cloot in vanitee, but ther is also costlewe furrynge in hir gownes, so muche pownsonynge of chisels to maken holes, so muche daggynge of sheres; forthwith the superfluitee in lengthe of the forseide gownes, trailynge in the dong and in the mire, on horse and eek on foote, as wel of man as of womman, that al thilke trailyng is verraily as in effect wasted, consumed, thredbare, and roten with donge, rather than it is yeven to the povre, to greet damage of the forseyde povre folk.[34]

According to the Parson's simple but accurate formula, this sort of conspicuous consumption damages the poor: "the moore that clooth is wasted, the moore moot it coste to the peple for the scarsnesse."[35] And even if the cloth were saved, it would still be worthless for common folk: "And forther over, if so be that they wolde yeven swich pownsoned and dagged clothyng to the povre folk, it is nat convenient to were for hire estaat, ne suffisant to beete hire necessitee, to kepe hem fro the distemperance of the firmament."[36] These fur-trimmed, embroidered, notched clothes are grossly inappropriate, inadequate, and impractical for workers. Equally wasteful and impractical are luxurious riding clothes, showy riding equipment, and Pride of the Table: "excesse of diverse metes and drynkes, and namely swich manere bake-metes and dissh-metes, brennynge of wilde fir and peuynted and castelled with papir, and semblable wast, so that it is abusioun for to thynke."[37] Such habits leave Lazarus begging at Dives's door: "for certes, riche men been cleped to festes, and povre folk been put awey and rebuked."[38] In terms of both price and practicality, the Parson believes that extravagant clothes and food are sinful and absurd.

A 1362 petition from Commons that describes increasing prices and conspicuous consumption seems more concerned with maintaining the distinctions in appearance that signifed social status than with just controlling exhorbitant spending:

> because divers people of divers conditions use divers apparel not pertaining of their estate; that is to say, laborers use the apparel of craftsmen, and craftsmen the apparel of valets, and valets the apparel of squires, and squires the apparel of knights . . .poor women and others the apparel of ladies, poor clerks fur like the king and other lords; therefore the below-mentioned merchandise sells at greater prices than it was accustomed to, and the wealth of the kingdom is destroyed.[39]

This petition resulted in the 1363 sumptuary act, which tried to limit the extravagance of consumers. The act forbade servants and craftsmen to wear precious metals and stones, silk, embroidered clothing, and fur.[40] In terms of organization, the statute "proceeds in ascending social order, through knights and clergy" before it "finishes with an appendage limiting rustics to blanket cloth and russet, and grouping them with those who have less than forty shillings of property."[41] The addition of this provision suggests that even rustics might try to dress inappropriately for their *status*.

The 1362 petition's concern about destroying the "wealth of the kingdom" seems odd when we consider that the ostentation it criticizes is itself a sign of wealth. The implication is that such extravagance comes at the expense of the domestic economy, an assertion supported by the growing preference for foreign goods. England's paradoxical monetary shortage in the face of increasing per capita wealth was largely the result of the imbalance of trade and payments between northern and southern Europe that swelled by the second half of the fourteenth century. Miskimin goes so far as to declare a "structural dichotomy" between the trade of northern and southern Europe.[42] Products from the north, such as wool in England, "were typically heavy, bulky commodities of low value per unit; often they were raw or semifinished materials or food goods,"[43] while the south offered "more compact, luxurious, and varied goods" such as finished textiles, perfumes and spices, and ivory.[44] The low value of raw goods and the difficulty of shipping them at reasonable cost put northern countries like England at a distinct disadvantage when they engaged in international trade, which is one reason we see the English rapidly develop their finished woolen cloth industry in the second half of the fourteenth century.[45]

The tension between the domestic wool market and the foreign silk merchants provides one of the best illustrations of shifting consumer preference and its consequences. Miskimin describes the growing demand for silk as a luxury good at the expense of wool; while the higher clergy and nobles had long enjoyed silks, the market for luxury fabrics "deepened considerably" during the fourteenth century.[46] If silk were a domestic product, few of the English would have complained; the problem was that most of the luxury goods popular in England were from abroad, and England was not prepared monetarily to engage in international trade on such a scale. While English merchants in the early fourteenth century traded in silver, Italian merchants "enjoyed a bimetallic monetary system from the middle of the thirteenth century along with advanced credit systems," which "tended to economize the metallic currrency."[47] Because the English remained dependent on precious metals, eventually including gold, they were vulnerable to the monetary shortages that an imbalance of trade can trigger.

In addition to increasing domestic consumption of foreign goods, the growing demand for luxury goods decreased domestic production for export as the domestic skilled labor force increased production of luxury goods, which exerted pressure on the local labor markets such that "labor was pulled toward the production of such finery for home consumption" and "withdrawn or pre-empted from the manufacture of exportable goods that might have competed for the luxury markets of the world."[48] As luxury items such as embroidered silks grew in popularity, more labor shifted to the manufacture of such goods in response to growing demand, but when Piers advises women about what is suitable work, he urges more practical labor:

> Summme shul sowe þe sak for shedyng of þe Whete.
> And ye louely ladies wiþ youre longe fyngres,
> That ye haue silk and Sandel to sowe whan tyme is
> Chesibles for Chapeleyns chirches to honoure.

> Wyues and widewes wolle and flex spynneþ;
> Makeþ cloþ, I conseille yow . . . .[49]

The cloth these women are supposed to make is not for export or a luxury market; instead, this wool and linen will make clothes for the poor.[50] Instead of embroidering for the market, the women should sew garments for the church, but only when they have time after they have sewn sacks to prevent the loss of grain that will help feed the poor. The agricultural and domestic work that Piers advocates is precisely the sort of work that brought less and less money to the countryside. The English countryside, which produced few luxury products, bore the burden of the nation's growing monctary shortages as increasing imports and decreasing exports heightened England's trade imbalance in a growing international market.

One of the chief economic effects of conspicuous consumption in fourteenth-century England and its resultant trade imbalance was the intensification of an already growing shortage of bullion and, by extension, coin. Such coin and bullion problems did not begin with the plague; N. J. Mayhew notes that the money supply in England was already showing signs of shortage at least thirty years preceding the Black Death.[51] In the first half of the fourteenth century, silver mining declined drastically as medieval mining techniques proved inadequate for older mines; as the silver mines became deeper, flooding frustrated attempts to gather ore.[52] The Devon silver mines, for example, produced no more than £70 of silver per year by 1347, a drastic decline from the mines' average of about £900 per year in the last decade of the thirteenth century.[53]

The initial response of the English crown to falling silver supplies was to try to keep English coin at home and to draw foreign coins to English mints for re-minting. In 1331 and 1335, ordinances "prohibited the export of English coins and ordered all foreign coins brought into England to be brought to the mint," and "[s]earchers were encouraged at sea-ports by the offer of a prize of one-third of any good money they found leaving the realm, or bad money they found coming in."[54] The 1331 ordinance promised serious consequences for the exportation of "good money": such a violation was punishable by death or forfeiture of all goods.[55] "Good money" usually referred to coins of the quality of ancient sterling, whose export was again prohibited in 1343.[56] In 1344, after England introduced gold coinage, a proclamation and ordinance prohibited persons from carrying either gold or silver out of the country except in the form of gold nobles.[57] Such money shortages continued through the plague period into the second half of the fourteenth century, and petitions or ordinances to prevent the export of money were frequent from mid-century until near its end.[58] Sometimes merchants faced import restrictions unless they imported a percentage of the value of their goods in bullion.[59] The only significant pause in complaints about money shortages seems to be from 1353 to 1363, which suggests that booty and ransoms flowed into England in the decade following the English military victories at Crecy and Poitiers.[60]

Mayhew cites several other reasons for a reduced coin supply, most of which refer to English silver passing out of domestic circulation. Coins might be scattered abroad or lost in hoards or shipwrecks. They might be clipped or so worn that reminting resulted in fewer coins. Some silver was also lost in the fire in the process of minting, so each reminting of old coins yielded fewer new ones. Finally, silver was drained from England not only by trade, but by war, diplomacy, and tribute to Rome.[61] The taxes raised to help cover the cost of the Hundred Years' War and the expenses entailed with maintaining a growing royal household and bureaucracy, payable in cash but not in kind, further drained silver from circulation, especially from the countryside. Even worse, the payments due to the court at Rome meant that bullion left the country for good. In 1366 Edward III prohibited the collection and transfer abroad of Peter's Pence, and a 1376 petition blames papal payments as a major cause of exported money.[62] Recurrent concerns in England with papal payments show up in 1376, 1384, 1399, 1409, and 1433.[63]

The main loss of bullion, according to Miskimin, was due to England's trade imbalances: "since a prime source of bullion was imported coin, a source which amounted to more than 90 per cent of total mint purchases in all but one of the years 1304–1325, coinage figures are directly related to the balance of payments."[64] To make matters worse, other northern European countries which had enjoyed a silver currency also began to trade more with the East, thus draining bullion from the area as a whole. Miskimin explains how the Eastern preference for silver[65] helps explain the increased commercial use and producton of gold coins in the West:

> The net result of an extensive commerce between East and West under these conditions would be similar to that produced by international arbitrage. Silver would drain from the West, and as it did the remaining gold would assume an increasingly

> important role as a monetary metal. The relative proportion of gold in western European coinages would increase, even though no gold were imported, as total coinage diminished in the face of an adverse balance of payments.[66]

To make matters worse, foreign traders often traded according to the weight instead of the face value of currency, and many old coins in circulation had deteriorated over the years. For this reason, light coins could be passed more easily at home, so "good money" was more likely to be sent abroad than clipped or rubbed coins.[67] The silver shortage made it difficult for the English to repair its worn coinage. Mayhew explains that reminting would have increased the coin shortage "unless the crown made up the difference between worn and new pence with an influx of new silver which it did not have the silver reserves to do."[68]

Without the silver to replace its lost coinage, England decided in 1343 to begin minting gold. Prestwich records that in 1339 Edward III rejected the idea of recognizing foreign gold coins as legal tender because he would thereby be "agreeing to the circulation in England of coins minted by his rival, Philip VI of France."[69] And despite the prohibition of foreign coins, florins and other gold coins were evidently in circulation in England already. Prestwich notes that records from before the English minted gold in 1344 show "the theft of florins, and of their being used to pay rents."[70] Furthermore, we know that gold coins were already in wide use because records from the 1344 gold purchases for the mint show that "the bulk of it was in the form of French coins, rather than bullion or plate."[71]

Whether one has a newly minted coin or a clipped or worn one makes no difference in an economy where the currency always circulates at face value, just as it makes no difference whether our paper bills are torn or not. But in the Middle Ages, many countries applied more than one standard value, and which standard applied depended largely on political strength. Only a strong government can enforce a face value, or par value, of an eroded currency based on bullion. A second standard value is the market rate for bullion; merchants who illegally weigh money instead of counting it measure currency's intrinsic value, the amount of bullion in the coins.[72] According to Miskimin, the English crown did not have the "political force to insist upon the legal tender value of the coinage and to decree circulation at par" until the end of the Middle Ages.[73] In times of political confusion such as near the end of the reign of Edward III and during most of the reign of Richard II, even domestic merchants would be tempted to demand illegal payment in weight and would thus demand higher prices in terms of face value.

Coin and bullion shortages together with the concentration of wealth helped widen the apparent gap between rich and poor in fourteenth-century England. While the rich spent exhorbitantly on foreign goods and embellished their clothing, riding tackle, utensils, and other gear with precious metals, those without money—not only the poor, but the cash poor, which is a crucial distinction when we consider the 1381 revolt—watched the stuff that comprises their currency squandered. When the same men who ostentatiously exhibited their wealth tried to squeeze even more cash out of the commons, the outcry was not limited to the rural poor, but heard from workers in a range of primary and secondary occupations.

The considerable economic upheaval of the fourteenth century—its money and labor shortages, changing demographics, shifting consumption patterns—left much of the upper class and growing middle class in England better off than they had been in the past. Some peasants even benefitted; with rising wages, laborers in greater demand, and cleared but uncultivated land in unprecedented supply, some laborers were able to acquire their own land.[74] We might then wonder why, with falling rents and rising wages, the English Uprising of 1381 erupted.

Advantages such as the ability to acquire one's own land were mixed blessings. A small landholder might be able to farm his holding with the help of his family, but a holding a little larger might require additional help at harvest. A new landholder with a small or medium-sized holding might not have the cash reserves to pay for additional help, while larger estates had the resources to attract temporary workers. Facing a labor shortage, rich peasant employers would have to offer higher wages than the lords of the manors with whom they had to compete.[75] If we note that the large landholders were often lords who still enjoyed labor services from the locals, we can imagine how tensions mounted as small holders were forced to ignore their own untilled or ripe fields to work for free for their competition. For those peasants whose labor services had been commuted to money rents, the stagnant grain market often provided insufficient cash for payments. And although all agricultural producers faced the difficulty of remaining solvent while trying to sell a cash crop at a good price during a money shortage, larger estates had established relationships with buyers while smaller landholders often had to try to sell to others like themselves who had no cash.

Another source of discontent stemmed from the reaction of large landholders as they tried to cope with the changing labor situation and grain market. Not all of the landlords' actions focused on squeezing labor. Some landlords diverted land from production of cheap grains for primary consumption to those for secondary consumption in the production of products such as beer, wine, or dyes, and other producers switched from "labor-intensive to land-intensive cultivation," such as herding.[76] In addition to such practical measures, some lords tried to reinstate or create new labor services such as carting, plowing, and harvesting.[77] The greatest conflict between landlords and laborers arose from this "fairly general seigneurial reaction against inevitable attempts by tenants to take advantage of the changed land-labour ratio."[78] Widespread grievances erupted with attempts to enforce The Ordinance of 1349 and the Statute of Labourers (1351), which restricted workers' geographic mobility and forced all men younger than 60 years old to work at pre-plague wage rates that were significantly lower than the market demanded.[79] When the rebels met with Richard II outside London in 1381 they demanded the abolition of labor services and the new labor laws.

If labor laws were not bad enough to cause a revolt like the one in 1381, their administration was. The local justices who enforced such regulations with the help of their appointees were often the very landlords who benefitted from such legislation.[80] With their landlords as the Justices of Labourers or as Justices of the Peace, laborers rarely received just treatment. Such an arrangement directed anger at the courts and administrators of the government, a feeling only intensified by rising taxes, as Miskimin argues:

> The necessities of war finance rendered the repressive labor laws even less palatable; rights of purveyance, forced sales to the government at low prices, and increased taxation such as the series of poll taxes in the late thirteen-seventies further inflamed peasant sentiment against the intrusion in rural affairs of the central government on a novel scale.[81]

Compounding unrest was the fact that the landlord-justices often appointed local tax officials.[82] Hilton explains that such steadily increasing economic pressure "widened and generalized the responses of the ruled, the peasants in particular."[83] Even if the general standard of living for peasants improved during this time, rising taxes combined with poor chances of selling crops, falling earnings, and the rising costs of manufactured goods made the peasant subjectively worse off; compared with the growing luxury and standard of living in the towns, rural inhabitants were relatively worse off than before the plague. But while "the sharpest fiscal pressure of the century . . . bore directly and unequally on the poorest sections of the population,"[84] the fiscal pressures of wartime taxes in a time of money shortages were not limited to peasants in the countryside.

While this study focuses mainly on economic difficulties associated with agricultural areas, towns were certainly not exempt from injustice and the economic pressures of taxes and trade restrictions. W. M. Ormrod characterized the 1381 rising as indicative of "a serious loss of public confidence in the central administrative and legal departments located in Westminster Palace and the city of London and a general indictment on the inadequacy and corruption of their staff."[85] As often happened in the countryside, laws were not applied or enforced equally for all parties. In the towns, in addition to tax burdens, merchants faced stiff competition from foreign merchants, a condition which helps explain the xenophobic reaction of the rebels who attacked the Flemish clothmakers in London. Foreign merchants with ready cash could circumvent penalties imposed by ordinances that outlawed smuggling and limited bullion export, for example, more easily than domestic lawbreakers. In her study of events in London preceding the 1381 revolt, Pamela Nightingale recounts such an instance:

> The case of Nicholas Sardouche aptly explains why the mercers had taken law into their own hands. Sardouche was a Luccan merchant who was found guilty by a London jury of smuggling £6,000 worth of silks and spices into the realm and of illegally exporting gold and silver worth £1,000. He was also accused of forestalling luxury imports to the loss of the City's mercers and grocers. He was imprisoned, but for a fine of £200 the king pardoned him and on 25 June 1369 ordered the sheriffs to return his confiscated goods and not to molest him further.[86]

The case of this merchant is representative of the sort of special treatment of foreign traders and workers that apparently infuriated English natives, provoked their xenophobia, and culminated in the murder of the Flemish weavers. A case like that of Sardouche would confirm the allegations of both Langland and the 1381 rebels that Meed held the whole country sway. The widespread perversion of justice by wealthy lawbreakers, wealthy accusers, and wealthy justices appeared to extend all the way to the king, who was in just as tight a bind for wartime cash as the rest of the country. Lady Meed did hold sway from the country courts to the king, and we should therefore not be surprised to see the degree to which Langland explored the relationship between money and justice.

CHAPTER FOUR

Fellowship and Apocalypticism:
Piers Plowman and the Nature of Association

As an apocalyptic poem, *Piers Plowman* reveals Langland's sense of imminent social change as the medieval economy based on feudal association gives way to one based in mutual economic and political interest. The poem also reveals the poet's anxiety about the instability of traditional metaphors for religious experience given this social turbulence, especially when those metaphors rely on economic language and imagery. This chapter explores how the language of *Piers Plowman* not only reflects an economic and ideological crisis, but also exhibits a vocabulary in crisis, a language evolving in response to the challenges of proto-capitalism. In *Piers Plowman,* Langland resists the new profit economy and endorses an old feudal ideology in which Christian ethics govern notions of fellowship, from common companionship to formation of the State. In Will's struggle between economic necessity and voluntary poverty, the reader can detect the poet's worry as economic relations replace Christian brotherhood and feudal obligation as the ties that bind.

As the basis of fellowship and society in Langland's England shifted from feudal and religious obligation to common economic interest, the idealistic notion of society as a religous community working for the common good gave way to a system in which individual interests and desires determined one's associations. While the feudal system certainly addressed common economic interests, the shift toward the profit economy created a greater contrast between work performed for the common good and work done for individual gain at the expense of society, particularly to the detriment of the commons.

According to the *Middle English Dictionary*, the terms "fellowship" and "company" each shifted meaning late in the century so that they no longer indicated only friendship and brotherhood, but came to signify those who shared economic interests, most notably guildsmen.[1] By the middle of the fifteenth century, the terms often referred to craft fraternities and guilds, knightly orders, and ecclesiastical bodies. Today, the term "company" continues to signify both companionship and economically-motivated organizational bodies.

The distinction between incorporated social bodies and groups of individuals interacting with a common purpose is crucial in studying *Piers Plowman* because the poem's moral instruction centers around guidelines to unify society which apply to all human relations, from friendship to politics to economic exchange. Raymond Williams's commentary on the changing meaning over time of the term "society" is useful because today's readers tend to think of society as an abstract or incorporated body, while the word in the Middle Ages signified active companionship or friendly relations among individuals.[2]

Concurrent with the shifting denotations of "society" from active condition or interaction to self-conscious abstraction or organization, the terms "state" and "estate" evolved in the later Middle Ages from terms that signified active conditions to ones that denoted powerful political institutions and abstract embodiments of society. We by habit conceive of the estates as classes in an incorporated, stratified society, while, following the medieval sense of the word, we should think of an estate as a situation or state—as *status*, one's general condition in life as defined by one's work. In the feudal Middle Ages, an estate was thus less an abstract subgroup of society than a condition or moral designation that brought people into society or fellowship with those who were like them and shared common interests and concerns—most commonly, work. Medieval social action such as the 1381 English Uprising was thus, as Williams puts it, the result of "active unity in fellowship"—the means to earthly renovation for a conservative such as Langland, who expected a religous fellowship founded on Christian works and proper work, as well as for the rebels who adapted parts of *Piers Plowman* for their own purposes.

The need for people with similar conditions to interact with those in different states (e.g., laborers before a lord who demands money, goods, or more work) propelled the shift from state to estate, from society and fellowship as companionship at work to self-conscious fellowship with a corporate purpose. Paradoxically, by Langland's time the strata of society had begun to solidify ideologically, with similar living conditions and the concept of the estates beginning to engender classes, but at the same time, actual social mobility increased with the growth of the profit economy. By the time Langland wrote *Piers Plowman*, self-conscious identification with groups had apparently intensified. Sharing work, skills, and economic concerns enabled fraternities to develop from religious craft associations to more powerful guilds with civic representation. Craftsmen might even identify each other's affiliations by dress, as do Chaucer's guildsmen in the Prologue to the Canterbury Tales; the guildsmen "were clothed alle in o lyveree / Of a solempne and a greet fraternitee."[3] As the growth of the guilds attests, the motive for fellowship in late medieval England became increasingly economic. And as Chapter 3 details, the demographic upheaval of the fourteenth century intensified the population's desire and ability to accumulate wealth, an aspiration certainly not confined to merchants and usurers in the fourteenth century.

Growing concern with the moral and political danger of two economic extremes, hoarding and profligate spending, resonates in one of Langland's influences, *Wynnere and Wastoure*, in which two groups of warriors debate before a middle-aged Edward III. The poem not only depicts economic immoderation in the fourteenth century, but does so with apocalyptic urgency and reference. Like *Piers Plowman*, *Wynnere and Wastoure* surveys contemporary society and bemoans its moral degeneration and economic impropriety, which Gollancz identifies as "the problem of Economy and Waste."[4] As in *Piers Plowman*, the ties that once bound society together in mutual cooperation and interdependence for the common good no longer seem to hold. The poem begins with the narrator's expression of wonder at the corruption of contemporary society:

> Sythen that Bretayne was biggede, and Bruyttus it aughte,
> Thurgh the takynge of Troye with tresone with-inn,
> There hathe selcouthes bene sene in seere kynges tymes,
> But neuer so many as nowe by the nynde dele.
> For nowe alle es witt and wylle that we with delyn,
> Wyli workes and slee, and icheon wryeth othere;
> and now es no frenchipe on fere bot fayntnesse of hert.[5]

The poet's evaluation of his generation is immediately followed by an apocalyptic warning that pairs social degeneration and natural calamities as two major signals of the impending Day of Judgment:

> For-thi sayde was a sawe of Salomon the wyse—
> It hyeghte harde appone honde, hope I no noþer,—
> When wawes waxen schall wilde, and walles bene doun,
> And hares appon herthe-stones schall hurcle in hire fourme,

> And eke boyes of no blode, with boste and with pryde,
> Schall wedde ladyes in londe, and lede at hir will,
> Then dredfull domesdaye it draweth neghe aftir.
> Bot who-so sadly will see and the sothe telle,
> Say it newely will neghe, or es neghe here.[6]

The disruption of feudal order accomplished when "boys of no blode" marry "ladyes" and then "lede at hir will" has both economic and political consequences. Assuming a sort of work inappropriate to their *status*, such boys violate social order; their mariages become signs of Doomsday because they signal in a more general sense that society is out of order. Affirming traditional economic and social categories, Langland and the poet of *Wynnere and Wastoure* clearly distinguish between "kinds" of men. We see the work such boys are fit for later in the poem when the Winners urge the Wasters to teach their men to till and fence the fields or risk the judgment of God:

> Owthere hafe as þou haste done, and hope aftir werse—
> Þat es firste þe faylynge of fode, and then the fire aftir,
> To brene the alle at a virre, for thi bale dedis:
> The more colde es to come, als me a clerke tolde.[7]

The Wasters are drunken profligates much like Langland's Wasters from Passus V. The Winners include the court, clergy, and merchants, all of whom accumulate and store material wealth. Most of the Winners of the earlier poem would be classified by Langland as Wasters unless they gave to the needy from their stores. Both companies in *Wynnere and Wastoure* have surplus wealth, and the poor do not figure into the debate except as ammunition for the Wasters' attacks; for example, the Wasters admonish the Winners: "Late the peple and the pore hafe parte of thi siluer."[8] The king seems politically savvy and content to have both groups of kinsmen at his service at home and abroad, but he seems as overcome by the workings of Meed as Langland's king in Passus V.

Neither *Piers Plowman* nor *Wynnere and Wastoure* offers a practical or worldly program to reform a society corrupted by material wealth. Instead, each poem awaits apocalyptic intervention to lead the way out of the current crisis. Compared to the cynical satire of *Wynnere and Wastoure*, in which everyone might be damned and in which the king happily accepts both morally suspect groups for his own political and economic purposes, Langland's apocalyptic view is more hopeful; at least in *Piers Plowman* the king may resist corruption and attempt to rule with Reason and Conscience.[9] And while the struggle between Antichrist and Holy Church at the end of the poem is unresolved, Christian doctrine would assure Langland and his readers of the eventual triumph of Truth in the person of Christ the King himself.

Christian and apocalyptic conceptions of society and fellowship clearly divide humanity into two camps in the afterlife; one is either in the company of God and the saints or in the company of the devil and sinners. Although on earth one is inclined to both good and evil, one's actions and companions here determine one's place in the afterlife. Those who seek salvation must not only live according to Christian values, but must separate themselves from the company of immoral folk unless attempting to reform them. This separation is asserted by Paul in 2 Corinthians:

> Bear not the yoke with unbelievers. For what participtation hath justice with injustice? Or what fellowship hath light with darkness? And what concord hath Christ with Belial? Or what part hath the faithful with the unbeliever? And what agreement hath the temple of God with idols? For you are the temple of the living God; as God saith: *I will dwell in them, and walk among them; and I will be their God, and they shall be my people*. Wherefore, *Go out from among them, and be ye separate*, saith the Lord, *and touch not the unclean thing*.[10]

A similar passage in 1 John characterizes the means of obtaining fellowship with Christ as a decision to walk in the light, which is directly connected with avoiding lies, admitting one's sins, and seeking forgiveness.[11]

One's fellows are clear indicators of one's moral condition. By the late fourteenth century, a "fellow" could be a wedded mate or a prostitute, a brother in Christ or an associate in crime,[12] with the morality of each fellowship determined by the character and actions of its members. Although people may fall into fellowship by chance, as Chaucer would have us believe his pilgrims do, the decision to continue such company has both moral and political implications. The moral danger of falling in among "false" friends is clear in Chaucer's *Friar's Tale*, in which we see the consequences of welcoming the worst companions and the direct results of allying oneself with the devil. When the dishonest summoner in *The Friar's Tale* is greeted by the devil, he replies, "Welcome . . . and every good felawe!"[13] The irony, of course is that this is no "good" fellow at all, but the fiend; but because "like associates with like," a "good felawe" for the summoner is paradoxically evil and corrupt. Bad company, then as now, could entice a new fellow to evil deeds, and even if he avoided wrongful action of his own, he could still remain in peril of a sin of omission for failing to work against the sinful intentions of his companions.

True company and false company, the sheep and goats of Judgment Day, embody the moral rift that apocalyptic narratives seek to mend, and Langland's poem is no exception. Langland employs the term "felawshipe" to show the moral peril of association and to illustrate the apocalyptic dichotomy between good and evil. When Langland describes the initial rift in holy society, he tells us that Lucifer traded in life with God for the society of fiends and "fel fro þat felawshipe in a fendes liknesse"[14] because "he brak buxomnesse."[15] All men thus either live in light or darkness, with true friends or false fiends like themselves. In *Piers Plowman*, those in fellowship with each other are most likely to be of the same general state, sharing work, living conditions, and common concerns.

The penetration of Unity Holy Church by the Antichrist friars at the end of *Piers Plowman* is ironic, for the type of brotherhood ideally shared by clerics such as friars, assuming they are not corrupt, is the sort of fellowship on which Christian society is based. The corrupt fellowship of the friars in Langland's poem is particularly detrimental to his vision of Unity because such friars are supposed to exemplify the very type of Christian brotherhood and poverty they undermine. In a passage friars often used as a scriptural basis for their order,[16] Jesus ordains his disciples and sends them out two by two, each with a fellow. The two friars who penetrate Unity in Passus XX are described as a "frere and his felawe,"[17] just as the greedy friar in Chaucer's *Summoner's Tale* is accompanied by a *felawe* who carries wax writing tablets to record what they collect and who travels ahead to arrange comfortable accommodations while his *felawe* works on getting more money.[18] These friars are obviously not what Jesus or Francis had in mind,[19] for the corrupt friars of Langland's poem come complete with crammed bags and purses, the attibutes of greed. Not the friars, but Piers plants both physical food and the spiritual seeds of Prudence, Temperance, Fortitude, and Justice,[20] while degenerate friars and their associates run in packs like Langland's personified vices.

When Langland characterizes perversions of charity and justice in *Piers Plowman*, he depicts them as companions to each other: Fals and Fauel, Gyle and Lyere, Symony and Civil, the Seven Deadly Sins. These personified detriments to charitable society travel in packs like Lucifer's legions, and Langland uses "felawship" to describe the relationship of Falsnesse and his "feeres."[21] Their effects can be seen both within estates, such as when household members argue or backbite,[22] and also between them, such as when the temporal and religious estates cheat the commons. Langland clearly adheres to the principle that one becomes like one's fellows and that good and evil cannot by nature mix. When the dreamer asks the friar in Passus VIII where *dowel* and *do yuele* both dwell, the friar responds that they both dwell with the friars. The dreamer objects because "dowel and do yuele mowe noȝt dwelle togideres."[23]

The complementary ideas that "like associates with like" and that "opposites cannot be joined" are not only practical and religious, but metaphysical. In Boethius's *De Consolatione Philosophiae*, Lady Philosophy answers questions about the nature of all things and the Providence of God. Divine thought, which regulates all things, she declares simple and stable. But temporal man is subject to Destiny or Fate, which disposes what Providence has knitted together. All things under Destiny are joined in the center and revolve around the point identified as the center of things, God. Chaucer translates:

> yif ther be any thing that knytteth and felawschipeth hymself to thilke myddel poynt, it is constreyned into simplicite . . . and it ceseth to ben schad and to fleten diversely; ryght so, by semblable reson, thilke thing that departeth ferrest fro the first thought of God, it is unfolden and summittid to grettere bondes of destyne.[24]

The more closely anything is bound to the center, the less it is subject to the instability of fortune. Those who are *felawes* to the light and the dark are in two different orbits; those who are closest to the center light, God, are bound more closely to God, and because they live simple lives constrained by God's laws, they conform to the will of God, Providence. Those *felawes* in the outer circles receive less light and are not bound in their orbit as securely; they are more likely to be subject to Fate than are the steadfast.

But in the world of *Piers Plowman,* much of the clergy, who should be close to the center, are far from God; in this world, a simple plowman represents the pope and occupies the inner circle, while the rest of society whirls out of control. The job of retaining order and measure in the universe, on earth, and in society is assigned to the figure of Nature—*Kynde* in *Piers Plowman*, a figure of the same philosophic and poetic lineage as Chaucer's Nature in the *Parlement of Foules* and Boethius's Lady Philosophy. Lady Philosophy consistently maintains the polarity of good and evil, even when she answers the question,

"Why do good things come to bad people?" She makes it clear that wealth, power and goodness are not necessarily joined because goods and power are not intrinsically good or evil:

> And yit moreover, yif it so were that thise dygnytes or poweris hadden any propre or naturel goodnesse in hemself, nevere nolde they comen to schrewes. For contrarious thynges ne ben nat wont to ben ifelachiped togydre. Nature refuseth that contrarious thynges ben ijoygned. And so, as I am in certeyn that ryght wykkyd folk han dignytees ofte tyme, thanne scheweth it wel that dignytees and poweres ne ben nat gode of hir owene kynde, syn that they suffren hemselve to cleven or joynen hem to schrewes.[25]

Goods and power are not necessarily good or bad in themselves, just as Meed can represent both legitimate pay and illegitimate reward. What the evil man debases is not the nature of the goods or power, but himself. Just as Lucifer's heavenly nature fell to that of a devil, the nature of man falls to the nature of a beast.

Lady Philosophy tells us that when men become *schrewes*, "gret peyne felawschipith and folweth hem!"[26] She argues that because all things that are good are one, those who are not good cease to be, which is not very convincing when Boethius is still bound to lose his life. Philosophy asserts that evil men become lesser creatures:

> [W]han thei ben perverted and turned into malice, certes, thanne have thei forlorn the nature of mankynde . . . . schrewes, whiche that schrewednesse hath cast out of the condicion of mankynde, ben put undir the merit and the dissert of men. Than betidith it that, yif thou seest a wyght that be transformed into vices, thow ne mayst nat wene that he be a man.[27]

A list of vices follows, and Philosophy associates people who indulge in each vice with various animals, such as the avaricious, voracious wolf and the angry lion.

The trope of bestial degeneration or transformation, marked not only by the loss of reason and language but of ontological status on the Chain of Being as well, is at least as old as the Book of Daniel, in which we find the most significant biblical expression of the trope. In Daniel, God punishes Nebudchadnezzar for his excessive pride just as he punished Lucifer: by reducing him to a lesser creature.[28] When the fourteenth century author of *Cleanness* retells the tale, he stresses the king's beastly transformation and loss of reason as a punishment for acting unreasonably. Responding to Nebudchadnezzar's boasts, the "Souerayn saȝe" sounds in his ears and silences him:

> Now Nabugodenozar innoȝe hatz spokken,
> Now is alle þy pryncipalte past at ones,
> And þou, remued fro monnes sunes, on mor most abide
> And in wasturne walk and wyth þe wylde dowelle,
> As best, byte on þe bent of braken and erbes,
> With wroþe wolfes to won and wyth wylde asses.[29]

Cast out of human society, wandering in the wilderness as punishment for his desire to put himself above all others,[30] the king loses his ability to reason along with his status as a human:

> His hert heldet vnhole; he hoped non oþer
> Bot a best þat he be, a bol oþer an oxe.
> He fares forth on alle faure, fogge watz his mete,
> And ete ay as a horce when erbes were fallen;
> Þus he countes hym a kow þat watz a kyng ryche,
> Quyle seuen syþes were ouerseyed, someres I trawe.[31]

The poet then amplifies the Biblical report of the king's bestial transformation, elaborately describing the king's, matted fur, bristly brows, eagle-claw nails, and beard extending to the ground.[32]

Kin of the wildman Nebudchadnezzar, the wildmen of the romances grow long hair and nails and usually wander bereft of reason. Some forge relationships with animals, their new companions, as both the misshapen giant of the woods and Ywayn do in the romance *Ywayn and Gawayn.* The giant is a foul creature "out of mesure," a "carl of Caymes kyn," a speaking beast who wears a strange garment of neither wool nor linen and who controls the beasts of the forest through pain and fear.[33] In his work on Chretien's *Yvain, ou le chavalier au lion*, Eugene Vance notes that the double title points up a "'special' relationship between a man and his generic animality."[34] Exploring the topic "from kind," Vance asserts that such a "man-beast is more *sub*ethical than he is evil, to the extent that his generic being is ontologically prior to the human species (understood as the perfection of animate creatures) exactly as the forest is prior to the ethical perfection of the court."[35]

Although Vance accurately claims that animals are ontologically prior to humans according to the medieval Christian view, the man-beast is not ontologically prior, but subsequent to the human species: he is a fallen, degenerative creature, and his regression results from immoderate feeling or sinful action. The common appellation "kin of Cain" given to man-beasts indicates that they are not *sub*ethical, but *un*ethical creatures, who debase and corrupt their human nature. Such beings do not revert to the amoral status of animals, but retain moral responsibility for their actions, however beastly. Just as Ywayn still remembers how to use a bow and the giant can speak and inflict purposeful cruelty to gain power, a human rather than animal drive, a man-beast still retains some human characteristics, motives, and responsibilities. *Ywayn and Gawayn* demonstrates that noble men who degenerate into man-beasts retain elements of their nobility and naturally become the fellows of noble beasts.[36]

In addition to the bestial degeneration of humans as a punishment for immoderation and sin in Daniel and *Ywayn and Gawayn*, we can see Chaucer employ the trope of bestial degeneration in the *Knight's Tale*. Throughout the *Knight's Tale*, Chaucer uses the term "felawe" to characterize the relationship between Palamon and Arcite, but when the loyalty between these sworn brothers breaks down, when they are no longer noble *felawes*, they too are transformed into beasts who share only the fellowship of instinct. Before Theseus comes upon them and halts their uncontrolled battle, the kinsmen are described as mad lions, cruel tigers, wild boars.[37] The next two times Palamon uses the word *felawe*,[38] he asks for Theseus to slay Arcite as well as himself, signifying their new bond of destruction.

In *Piers Plowman*, one process by which man becomes the fellow of beasts and degenerates to a beast himself is through immoderate desire and association with Lady Meed. She and her fellows ride a sheriff, a juror, summoners, Deans, Archdeacons, and various other officials who are saddled with silver with which to bribe bishops into condoning sins including usury.[39] Similarly, in the society out of order in the Prologue, the humans are reduced to cats of the court, more than a thousand small mice, and a "route of Ratons."[40] This degeneration is based not on desire for Meed, but on desires, plans, and actions improper to one's status. The cat, who unjustly wields power over the rodents, who "lauȝte hem at will / And pleide wiþ hem perillousli and possed aboute,"[41] makes the rodents his victims, and while the rodents call their council "for commune profit,"[42] their deliberations belie that motive: "Miȝte we wiþ any wit his [the cat's] wille wiþstonde / We myȝte be lordes o lofte and lyuen at oure ese."[43] Hoping to bell the cat and thereby to live as lords, neither of which is appropriate to their station, the rodents are deterred not by the improper nature of their plans, but by practical considerations in the face of the cat's tyrannical power and by the knowledge that if they bell or destroy one cat, another will take its place. Belling a cat is not the prerogative of mice, but illustrates the immoderate and inappropriate desire of the commons, just as the cat's tyrannical behavior is immoderate and inappropriate for a just ruler. Yet the tyranny of a cat and the powerlessness of the rodents is perfectly natural for animals; Langland appears to suggest that when humans debase themselves, their animalistic behavior makes them vulnerable to the ravages of the natural order.

The ontological degeneration of humans into animals betrays *Kynde Wit*—a representation of Human Nature in Langland's scheme. Made in the image of God, men are set apart from the rest of Nature (*Kynde*) by their ability to reason; when they are unreasonable or degenerate morally, when they act against the dictates of God and Kynde, they devolve into lower types creatures types: animals. While all animals are classified by Kynde according to their own nature, their kind, man's ability to think and speak adds *Wit* to *Kynde*.

When Hugh White traces Kynde Wit from passus to passus, he recognizes its role at the foundation of human activity and notes that it "lies at the base of several aspects of society" including food procurement, the political system, law, morality, and society's division into estates.[44] White then questions why Langland examines the "fundamental structures of society" when the "*aims* of society could be articulated without any reference to Kynde Wit." One likely reason *Piers Plowman* explores the basis of human nature and society to the degree it does is that, for a Christian as conservative as Langland, the *aim* of Christian and feudal society is not in question; the *means* by which to realize those aims when the social structures supporting the system are rotting away is another problem, one central to the poem's investigations.

According to Langland, all human society should be governed by Kynde Wit, which binds people to reasonable action, and therefore even pagan societies are able to develop laws and moral standards by using reason. In *Piers Plowman*, Kynde Wit signifies not only human nature, but the body of knowledge that such a nature makes possible. Of course, Langland reminds the reader that this type of knowledge is nothing compared to the knowledge Christian revelation offers:

> For alle hir kynde knowyng com but of diuerse siȝtes.
> Patriarkes and prophetes repreueden hir science
> And seiden hir wordes ne hir wisdomes was but a folye;

As to þe clergie of crist counted it but a trifle:
Sapiencia huius mundi stulticia est apud deum.[45]

The "kynde knowyng" one can accumulate with Kynde Wit is limited to reasonable observation, usually of natural phenomena. No amount of natural observation, however, can bring a man to Christianity:

No moore kan a kynde witted man, but clerkes hym teche,
Come for al his kynde wit to cristendom and be saued;
Which is þe cofre of cristes tresor, and clerkes kepe þe keyes
To unloken it at hir likyng, and to þe lewed peple
ȝyue mercy for hire mysdedes, if men wole aske
Buxomliche and benigneliche and bidden it of grace.[46]

Christian revelation and clergy's administration of sacramental grace, especially in the forgiveness of sins, is necessary mediation for the *lewed* to be saved.

When people, pagan or Christian, do not act according tọ Reason, which should "naturally" prescribe moderation according to the dictates of Kynde, they become "unkynde," both in nature and in deed. When the figure of Kynde comes to the dreamer with a vision of nature, he reveals the condition of fallen mankind as well:

Man and his make I myȝte se boþe.
Pouertee and plentee, boþe pees and werre,
Blisse and bale boþe I seiȝ at ones,
And how men token Mede and Mercy refused.
Reson I seiȝ sooþly sewen alle beestes,
In etynge, in drynkynge and in engendrynge of kynde.[47]

The dreamer then sees all of creation working according to Reason with the exception of mankind, whose immoderation when God and Nature provide enough for everyone is what causes the conditions of poverty and plenty, peace and war:

Ac þat moost meued me and my mood chaunged,
That Reson rewarded and ruled alle beestes
Saue man and his make; may tyme me þouȝte
No Reson hem ruled, neiþer riche ne pouere.[48]

Wit and Reason are not identical here. Reason in *Piers Plowman* refers to the faculty that moderates the appetites, that enables men to act reasonably. Langland does not employ Kynde Wit, as White claims, to validate the social structure,[49] but to designate the moral baseline below which humans no longer merit the fellowship of men, but of beasts like themselves.

Although some of the Seven Deadly Sins in Passus V receive absolution more readily than others, Langland labels Avarice, the sin that reduces those in Meed's retinue to animals, a particularly "unkyndly creature,"[50] and Repentance refuses absolution until Avarice performs penance. Reason is to record in the Register of Heaven that Avarice has made restitution in goods to all men he harmed and fulfilled the demands of the last stage of penance, satisfaction; the practice of restitution, however, was complicated in this period by changing economic relations and changes in how confessors determined individual penances, as Chapter 2 discusses in more detail.

Langland maintains that people can be *unkynde* not only by refusing to moderate their physical desires, but by failing to limit their intellectual inquiries. After he is confronted with the vision of Kynde, the dreamer reflects and rebukes Reason for not preventing man from misdeeds. Reason then scolds the dreamer for meddling in what is not his business. When people are unreasonable, when they are *unkynd*e either in physical desire or in their desire to know too much, they debase their nature. When men exercise Wit without the moderation of reason, they may try to know and discuss God's *pryvetee.* Clergy rebukes Will for such attempts:

> Adam, whiles he spak noȝt, hadde paradis at wille,
> Ac whan he mamelede about mete, and entremetede to knowe
> The wisedom and þe wit of god, he was put fram blisse.
> And riȝt so ferde Reson bi þee; þow wiþ rude speche
> Lakkedest and losedest þyng þat longed noȝt to doone;
> Tho hadde he litel likyng for to lere þe moore.[51]

Here we see the interdependence of speech and Kynde Wit. Just as Wit can be perverted, speech can be perverted along with it; in fact, Langland identifies speech as a cause of the Fall. Once Adam began to prate about God's wisdom, God banished him, just the fate Langland predicts for those who prate about the Trinity when its secrets belong to God and not man.

Although Reason is basic to human nature and links man to God through the application of order and moderation, Wit is as morally neutral as Meed. When

Wit is separated from Kynde, it loses all moderation, as we see in the personifications of warreners Witty and Wisdom at court with Lady Meed. When they first appear in Passus IV, Witty is described as Wisdom's "feere," his companion; they accompany each other because witty speech usually accompanies a wise facade. Conscience sees them as he is fetching Reason to the court, but he makes Reason ride away quickly because he knows that the pair "loued coueitise."[52] Conscience warns Reason:

> Ther are wiles in hire wordes, and with Mede þei dwelleþ;
> Theras wraþe and wranglynge is þer wynne þei siluer,
> Ac þere is loue and leautee hem likeþ noȝt come þere.[53]

Although Witty and Wisdom can argue either for Truth or Falsehood, just as Meed can be good or bad, we only see them in their debased forms in *Piers Plowman*, working for Meed as Wrong bids them instead of working for the Truth. When Wit and speech are perverted, justice can be corrupted along with them, which we see in Passus IV when Witty and Wisdom try to pay Peace and later bribe the king with Meed for Wrong's sake. When Reason records the deception of Meed in the court, Kynde Wit agrees, and the order of the court is restored as the king judges against Meed and her party. The commons call Meed a whore, and control is restored to the king, who promises to submit himself to the counsel of Reason and Conscience. Langland thus reaffirms the authority of the king while asserting that the king is subject to the same rule by Reason as all others. Restoring the king's control and authority, Langland reveals his hopes for reformed society, a vision more reactionary than revolutionary in character.

The suggestion of order at the end of the vision of the king's court is undermined, however, by the flight of Meed's retinue when she is apprehended. Falseness flees to the friars; Guile runs to the merchants; Liar shifts fellowship to pardoners, doctors, grocers, minstrels, messengers, and anyone else who would have him.[54] While Meed is scrutinized at court, these personified vices freely roam the kingdom. The friars also fetch away Fair Speech and dress him as a friar,[55] so we should be suspicious in Passus XX when *Hende speche* convinces Peace to let in "Þe frere and his felawe."[56] When Friar Flatterer, the false physician, penetrates *Unitas* and offers Contrition a less biting plaster for "a pryuee paiement,"[57] we learn that Meed's companions are still at work. As Peace says, "[T]he frere wiþ his phisyk þis folk haþ enchaunted."[58] If this were not enough to make the reader wary of the suggestion of a reformed society in Passus I–V, we should remember that even with Reason and Conscience in court, the king first sided with Meed.[59]

The vision of Meed and the court reiterates and allegorizes Holy Church's warning against covetousness in Passus I, in which Langland tenders his ideal vision of ordered society. After Holy Church presents this vision of true society, the dreamer requests that Holy Church teach him "by som craft to know þe false."[60] Holy Church tells him to look to his left, indicating the side to which those in the corrupt court—the goats—will be relegated at the Final Judgment, and the dreamer at once sees Lady Meed and her entourage. In addition to identifying Meed and her retinue as belonging to the company of the damned, such a division adds apocalyptic urgency, for it suggests that the process of separation and judgment has already begun. After Holy Church's warning, the dreamer should have recognized Meed at once as being on the wrong side, but instead, her appearance dazzles him despite the warning, just as the bushels of florins dazzle the rioters of Chaucer's *Pardoner's Tale* despite the old man's warning that death waits under the tree.[61] Even when signs show that what will follow are undeserved wealth, false fellowship, and death, the dreamer is attracted to Meed.

Although Meed is not intrinsically good or evil, Langland stresses her natural tendency toward evil, as we can see from her lineage and array of companions. In contrast with procreative marriage as a model of ideal fellowship, Meed is bad fruit engendered by false fellowship. Holy Church warns that Meed is a bastard child of False, and that she is like her father: "Qualis pater talis filius: Bon[a] arbor bonum fructum facit."[62] This Meed is not "of Amendes engendred,"[63] as she should be, but is of a different nature altogether. Meed is thus closely identified with the sinful fruit of Eden and those who partake of her can expect to lose their place in paradise.

The good fruit in *Piers Plowman*, both physical and spiritual, is not engendered by Meed, but planted and nurtured by God and by Piers. The good tree is not the tree of Meed, but the tree of Patience, which grows in the garden God planted in man and produces the fruits of Charity.[64] We are told that Jesus is going to his crucifixion on a tree to fetch from the fiend the fruit of Piers,[65] which is both the ultimate fruit of charity grown in the body of man and the symbol of man's redemption. The righteous fruit that the fiend has held captive in hell before the harrowing, the "fruit of Piers" who died before Christ, wait in the lap of Abraham, and Christ must harrow hell to make his fellowship more perfect, more complete. The imagery of the harvest and its prefiguration of the Final Judgment heightens the apocalyptic drama of these passages; just as the dreamer waits with the world for Christ's Resurrection on Easter and witnesses the harvest of the harrowing, the world waits for Christ's Second Coming and the final harvest.

The end of the B-text of *Piers Plowman*, in which Antichrist intrudes on the barn that is Holy Church, recalls an apocalyptic passage from 1 Corinthians in which Paul describes the foundation of Christ's Church as communal labor, as tending a farm and constructing a building in preparation for final judgment:

> I have planted, Apollo watered, but God gave the increase. Therefore, neither he that planteth is any thing, nor he that watereth, but God that giveth the increase. Now he that planteth, and he that watereth, are one. And every man shall receive his own reward, according to his own labour. For we [preachers and evangelists] are God's coadjutors: you are God's husbandry; you are God's building. According to the grace of God that is given to me, as a wise architect, I have laid the foundation; and another buildeth thereon. But let every man take heed how he buildeth thereupon. For other foundation no man can lay, but that which is laid; which is Christ Jesus. Now if any man build upon this foundation, gold, silver, precious stones, wood, hay, stubble: Every man's work shall be manifest; for the day of the lord shall declare it, because it shall be revealed in fire; and the fire shall try every man's work, of what sort it is.[66]

Acording to Paul, the clergy deserves no personal glory for their work, for God deserves all credit for the growth of His crops and building: His Church. As God's coadjutors, the clergy enter into a relationship of mutual help and cooperation with each other and God. Just as the clergy will be judged by their works, so will "every man" who builds on the foundation of Christ with whatever sort of works and materials he finds available. On Judgment Day, a man who built on the foundation of Jesus with materials consumed by fire will "suffer loss; but he himself shall be saved, yet so as by fire."[67] Salvation, then, is for all Christians who perform good works according to their lot, regardless of *status*. Although hay and stubble will burn, the work of building with them is sufficient for salvation. Similarly, Langland asserts throughout *Piers Plowman* that all people must work according to their ability in order to prepare for individual judgment by helping build, repair, and preserve Holy Church.

The distinction between good and bad, between heavenly and sinful fruit, is fully realized in the poem's distinction between spiritual and material wealth. In his article "Spirituality and Economics in Passus 1–7 of the B Text," James

camps of fellows, with Lady Meed leading one side and Piers the other. Just as honest fellowship leads to holy society, acts and associations motivated by envy and covetousness lead to destructive anti-fellowships. Most people live between holy society and wicked association in a maze of moral confusion, including the king, the narrator, and Hawkin, who all have to choose between true and false fellowship.

When Holy Church identifies herself, the dreamer cries for grace, for prayers for his sins, and to be taught *kyndely* to believe in Christ:

> 'Teche me to no tresor, but tel me þis ilke,
> How I may saue my soule þat Seint art yolden.'
> 'When alle tresors arn tried treuþe is þe beste.'[79]

Holy Church praises Truth and presents Love in the person of Jesus as the example by which to live, the model for Christian society. She counsels the rich to provide for the poor, for the rich will earn reward in heaven in the same measure they give here.[80] True treasure on earth is thus charitable, voluntary poverty. As Passus I ends, Holy Church rails at covetous clergy for their chastity without charity and reaffirms love and truth as the means to heaven. Setting spiritual treasure sharply against material accumulation allows Langland to set true treasure against false gain and to distinguish between those who seek each.

For Langland's dreamer and his fellow Christians, however, the challenge is not merely to keep from falling into *unkyndenesse*, but to be transformed into Paul's "new man," whom we see in the figures of Piers and the Good Samaritan. Although Wrong can reduce humans to animals, the grace and truth of Christian revelation can elevate human nature. Instead of man separating his wit from his nature in a desire to know too much, the Christian life of Piers changes his very nature. While men already share the nature of God because of the *imago Dei* instilled in Adam at his creation, the elevation of human nature in the incarnation, God becoming man and sharing in human nature, made this potential transformation possible. Those who would become *felawes* of Jesus are bound to imitate him according to the rule of fellowship, "like associated with like," and they are thus transformed from creatures with Kynde Wit to *euene cristenes*, "fellow Christians," a term used throughout the Acts of the Apostles and the Epistles along with "fellow brothers" and "fellow prisoners" to signify the new society among Christians.

If the way to debase one's human nature is to act like an animal, the way to elevate it is to imitate Christ. Truly just and charitable men are much harder to find than selfish ones in *Piers Plowman*, and they have little company. Jesus, Piers, and the Good Samaritan "resemble" one another, but few men live up to their standards, and each of them ends up eventually travelling alone. The three sometimes overlap in the poem because they share the same life; because they share the same human nature, Jesus suffers in Piers's human armor. Because they both live lives of *caritas*, the Samaritan rides on the ass from Jericho to Jerusalem in Jesus' Palm Sunday path instead of towards Jericho as he does in the gospel account.

Just as those in the Middle Ages considered the entire universe as one hierarchy ordered by God, and just as Lucifer's expulsion from heavenly fellowship shows that even heavenly society, at the top of the hierarchy near God, has its guidlines or laws, Langland asserts that society on earth must be conducted according to law, ideally resulting in relations governed by *caritas* and, by extension, regulated by justice tempered with mercy:

> Forþi is loue ledere of þe lordes folk of heuene
> And a mene, as þe Mair is, bitwene þe commune & þe kyng;
> Right so is loue a ledere and þe lawe shape.[81]

These guidelines for society are not only for those who are in friendly fellowship, but for all relations within and between estates. According to such ethical standards, the clergy should act as a force for *caritas* and should remind the king and nobles of their obligations as protectors of the commons and the church; they should administer the sacraments to those in Christian fellowship and provide an example of right living; they should serve as mediators between secular society and the moral and religious tenets at its core. Civil laws and their implementation should be based on the common good, and *caritas* should serve as the intermediary between the king and the commons as the means to harmonious Christian society.

Although the king and the commons do not have the same social obligations, the guidelines each must follow have the same ultimate foundation. If the king or nobles are not acting for the common good, if they are cruel or unreasonable or capricious, society, especially among the commons, may become chaotic and fearful, as we see in Langland's fable of the rodents and the cat. And when the moral and religious foundation ordering society is threatened by an evolving market economy and the desire of individuals to accumulate wealth, the clerical and temporal abuses of power which Langland criticizes ensue, again threatening the common good.

The problem the dreamer and the poet consistently return to, however, is that they do not live in this blissful state, but in the fallen world. In an ideal society, *kynde loue* and truth together rather than fallible Kynde Wit regulate law and morality, but the promise of a reformed society based on love and free from Meed belongs to the apocalyptic era described in Passus II when weapons become agricultural tools and priests "dyngen upon Dauid eche day til eue."[82] One can only wonder to what extent Langland anticipated the 1381 Uprising, when agricultural tools were used as weapons, or whether he realized how the economic pressures of relatively low grain prices made it profitable for cash-starved agricultural workers to sell agricultural tools for their valuable metal to become weapons in the war with France, as chapter 3 of this study suggests.[83] The world Langland envisions is a world transformed from one that is economically geared toward war and motivated by profit to one that is geared toward agriculture and subsistence and motivated by charity. The narrator, Hawkin, and virtually all of society need to be re-formed to realize this Christian utopia, one that is figured in terms of labor: "Ac kynde loue shal come ȝit and Conscience togideres / And make of lawe a laborer."[84] In Langland's poem, ideal community is contingent on individual moral reform. If the good or evil nature of one's fellowship reflect one's personal *kynde*, then reformed individuals inevitably embody reformed society.

The poem presents three cumulative levels of right action, each prior level subsumed in each later level, for those who want to live in Truth: *dowel*, *dobet*, and *dobest*. The better one wishes to do as an individual, the more good works, the more social action, one must contribute to society. *Dowel*, whom Langland associates with faith, does what the law teaches, does not begrudge others,[85] and lives humbly in awe of God: "That dredeþ god, he dooþ wel; þat dredeþ hym for loue."[86] *Dobet*, whom Langland associates with hope, helps others if he can and does not fear the vengeance of the Lord;[87] he may help others by being a member of the clergy and preaching.[88] But *Dobest*, whom Langland associates with *caritas*, doles out justice and uses his time well to work for others; he pushes down the wicked when they rise.[89] According to Langland, to do best is to heal and to help, to give aid to and take care of both young and old.[90] *Dobest* never wastes speech,[91] like the *wastours*, but instead makes the words of the psalms his own.

Langland suggests that the closer one wants to come to Christian perfection, the harder one must work for social justice according to the dictates of *caritas*. To *dobest* the "new man" must work for social justice if he wishes, like Piers and the Samaritan, to imitate Christ. Langland represents the difficulty of living according to *caritas* in this sinful world in the figure of Hawkin and in the wandering hunt of the narrator for Piers. Piers, however, is rarely found; once he attains Christian perfection, not even those in Unity know where Piers is, perhaps because he is no longer of this fallen world. In the latter half of the poem, Piers seems to surface only in conflated images where he is united with Jesus and the Samaritan.

The difficulty of realizing earthly reform is also clear from the poem's lack of closure. At the end of Passus IV when we last see the king's court, the kingdom is still in danger, and Langland leaves the spiritual community at the end of the poem in jeopardy as well. Langland provides no easy solutions to the corrupting influence of the Antichrist friar. Will is left to continue his search for Piers, for all Christians can do is to continue to pursue Christian perfection until the King comes and asserts his authority, whether an English king who restores order or Christ the King.

Piers Plowman may end in turmoil because depicting the final triumph of Truth would remove both the kingdom and the poem's focus from the problems of this world, and thus shift all attention from the need for reform to the promise of a heavenly kingdom on earth. Such an ideal society and how to achieve it may have been incomprehensible in a time of profound economic and social upheaval. Or perhaps, for Langland, depicting Christ's return in so topical a poem would intrude on God's *pryvetee,* for God alone judges when to intervene in human history. Noting that Adam was "put fram blisse" because he "entremetede to knowe / The wisedom and þe wit of god,"[92] Langland would not presume to pass judgment by depicting contemporary sinners on Doomsday, nor would he presume that his society was the very last and thus predict God's direct intervention, the timing of which is clearly God's prerogative and not man's. Langland thus stops short of envisioning a transformed society, either spiritually or politically, at the end of the poem. Unable to imagine a way out of the crises of his day except through already existing economic and political structures, the poet reaffirms the feudal base of spiritual and political society as the means to reform and the path to salvation:

> No moore kan a kynde witted man, but clerkes hym teche,
> Come for al his kynde wit to cristendom and be saued;
> Which is þe cofre of cristes tresor, and clerkes kepe þe keyes
> To unloken it at hir likyng, and to þe lewed peple

> ȝyue mercy for hire mysdedes, if men wole aske
> Buxomliche and benigneliche and bidden it of grace.[93]

Through distinctions such as whether one is *lewed* or not, feudal Christianity arranges its social structure. In the feudal paradigm, divisions of *kynde* support distinctions of *status*; the belief that there are different kinds of men makes it possible to distinguish between those of different conditions, expectations, and abilities. *Status* and *kynde* therefore come to designate both what kind of person one is and what sort of work one should do.

Langland thus juggles two social paradigms that had long ago accommodated each other. According to the Christian spiritual or moral paradigm, two kinds of men, true and false, cut across occupational categories and eventually would be separated into two apocalyptic camps. According to the practical or political paradigm of feudalism, three basic sorts of men lived in balance, a balance attained when people performed their proper work for the common good. Performing true work indicated that a man was true—whether a noble knight, a holy member of clergy, or an honest plowman. Being true to one's kind thus entailed working in support of the existing social structure, and maintaining that structure gained moral import. In its assertion of the ethical imperative to work for the common good, *Piers Plowman* reaffirms feudal divisions of labor and earns Langland the label of religious and social conservative, an appellation shared by chroniclers who recorded the upheaval of Langland's day.

For traditional Christian thinkers such as Langland, Gower, and the chroniclers, the actions of the 1381 rebels betrayed the commons' responsibilities and reduced them to packs of animals. Freely employing the trope of degeneration, Knighton calls the rebel clutches "the mouths of the wolves"[94] and describes the exhausted, drunken crowd as "sleeping like slaughtered pigs."[95] According to Froissart, the mob moved through the streets of London following one another like beasts.[96] Walsingham goes so far as to characterize the rebels as demonic beasts:

> a most horrible shouting broke out, not like the clamour normally produced by men, but of a sort which enormously exceeded all human noise and which could only be compared to the wailing of the inhabitants of hell. Such shouts used to be heard whenever the rebels beheaded anyone or destroyed houses, for as long as God per-

> mitted their iniquity to be unpunished. Words could not be heard among their horrible shrieks but rather their throats sounded with the bleating of sheep, or, to be more accurate, with the devilish voices of peacocks.[97]

From the perspective of the literate clergy and nobility, those who rebelled refused to act according to *kynde*, both in terms of acting unnaturally violent and in terms of their refusal to work obediently in accordance with their status. By asserting that the rebel bands were largely composed of and led by rubes and rustics and by ignoring the involvement of wealthier participants, minor clergy, and townspeople,[98] the chroniclers could more easily dehumanize their subjects and discredit their actions.[99] The rebellion according to the chronicler is thus an act against *kynde* and social order—an unnatural betrayal of the patient obedience long considered the duty of the working commons, who were expected to deport themselves, in Langland's words, "buxomliche and benigneliche." By characterizing the commons' complaints and actions as out of *mesure*, both as unnaturally violent and as unnatural in the sense that the rebels sought to understand and control what was considered beyond their ability or place, the chroniclers can dismiss the rebels as unthinking brutes and can drown out their human voices with the metaphoric sounds of beasts. Bereft of human voice and reason, the rebels and their complaints were largely silenced.

CHAPTER FIVE

Reading and Rebellion:
Imagining Radical Change and the 1381 Revolt

We can see just how important even minor knowledge of *Piers Plowman* is to interpreting late-medieval rebel messages by observing the error of the Dieulacres Abbey chronicler, who lists "Per Plowman" himself among the 1381 rebels. Apparently unfamiliar with Langland's poem, the chronicler mistakes the literary, symbolic figure he finds—perhaps in a version of John Ball's letter to the Essex Commons, the address of Jakke Carter, or a similar rebel message now lost—for an actual rebel conspirator. In any case, the Dieulacres chronicler probably misread; apparently unfamiliar with *Piers Plowman*, he assumed that the rebel messages referred to a real person rather than to a literary, symbolic, or pseudonymic figure.

The error of the Dieulacres chronicler supports Anne Hudson's assertion that the letters of John Ball, "to one who knew nothing about Langland's poem, would be completely unintelligible."[1] But if this statement is true of the chroniclers, it is also true of the rebels. For John Ball's letters to make sense to the rebels, or at least to other rebel leaders, they had to have some crude knowledge of Langland's poem. Although the extent to which the rebels knew *Piers Plowman* firsthand was surely limited by illiteracy, even illiterate peasants could have listened to parts of the poem, and the reader's ability to pick and choose which portions of the poem to popularize was a valuable opportunity for those who wished to invoke the poem's apocalyptic fervor and call to reform while ignoring its conservative message. As this chapter will demonstrate, all the rebels needed to know of *Piers Plowman* to make rudimentary sense of the rebel communications was that it posited a dichotomy between the honest workman Piers and robbers like Hobbe and that the progression from *dowel* to *dobet* to *dobest* required greater action in each stage. In fact, the general population's inability to read *Piers Plowman* probably strengthened the poem's potential as a instrument of rebellion; out of context, the figure of Piers and movement from *dowel* to *dobet* to *dobest* could be assimilated into the ideological groundwork for a radical and violent uprising.

Knowing that the historical and political model for medieval Christians was salvific, invested with economic metaphors, and comprised of two societies, one of good and one of evil, we are not entirely in the dark when we try to explain how and why rebel leaders found appealing and useful a poem as socially conservative as *Piers Plowman.* The answers to such questions are found not in what the poem counsels, but in the ideological thrust of the material Langland draws from and synthesizes; the poem's apocalyptic framework—its promises of a restored society, laments over contemporary corruption and injustice, and promises of imminent punishment and reward—all resonated loudly enough to drown out Langland's call for a more sober approach to social reform.

In scrutinizing evidence concerning the demands of the 1381 rebels and their apocalyptic expectations, we can learn much about the actions and communications of the rebels from information we have about similar apocalyptic social movements in the Middle Ages. Surveying millenarian movements and establishing how medieval rebels and schismatics synthesized traditional religious material and contemporary circumstance, Norman Cohn describes how political movements harness the apocalyptic expectations and fears of the masses and demonstrates that apocalyptic expression and millenarian movements often marry religious fervor and local or national politics. Cohn explains that the most "volatile elements" in medieval society could be attributed to the chronic frustration, disorientation, and anxiety of the population,[2] the same sort of conditions that prevailed for decades preceding the 1381 revolt as the result of famine, plague, and the challenge that the changing economy posed for the Christian ethical base of the feudal economy.[3] These volatile elements often would explode when fueled by apocalyptic and millenarian belief; as Cohn explains, when "eschatological doctrines penetrated to the uprooted and desperate masses," such beliefs were often "re-edited and reinterpreted until in the end they were capable of inspiring revolutionary movements of a peculiarly anarchic kind"[4] Such movements, of course, spawn leaders, and from what we know about John Ball and the other rebels, their leaders fit the profile of traditional leaders of apocalyptic and millenarian movements. According to Cohn, a *propheta,* the leader of such a movement, "himself belonged to a distinctive social type which changed little down the centuries."[5] Often part of a "frustrated and rather low-grade intelligentsia" among whom "eschatological lore was not only studied and conserved but also edited and elaborated until it was fit to serve as a revolutionary ideology," *prophetae* were often members of the lower clergy, "eccentric members of the lower nobility," or obscure laymen,[6] descriptions which fit the eclectic group involved in instigating the 1381 Uprising. Given the typical involvement of various estates in millenarian and apocalyptic movements, we should not be surprised that the rebel bands of 1381 cut across the strata of society, from peasants and artisans to the lower clergy to the lower nobility.[7]

The urgent character of apocalyptic thought and its tendency to divide society into opposed groups of good and evil served rebel groups well, for in the apocalyptic framework, time is always short, deliverance is assured, and the battle is no longer for merely political or economic stakes, but of universal consequence. Cohn asserts that in times of upheaval, the old eschatology could become

> a coherent social myth which was capable of taking entire possession of those who believed in it. It explained their suffering, it promised them recompense, it held their anxieties at bay, it gave them an illusion of security—even while it drove them, held together by common enthusiasm, on a quest which was always vain and often suicidal.[8]

In attempting to set the events of the apocalyptic narrative in motion in their own historical contexts, often with their own bands taking the role of avengers, millenarian rebels could rouse the crowd to violent action in the name of God. With the ultimate goal of establishing justice and thus peace on earth, rebels could justify the murder of "fals" men and "traitors"—like Archbishop Sudbury—in the name of Truth.

Because both Langland and the 1381 rebels imagined change within the framework of feudal Christian ideology, even critics who note the savagery of the uprising often balk at labelling the rebels "revolutionary." Rossell Hope Robbins, for example, explains that "[i]t was not so much the [rebel] ideas which were revolutionary, but their application,"[9] and Richard Firth Green argues that "on this still inchoate political spectrum we would have to place the leaders of the Peasants' Revolt firmly to the right."[10] In the same way that Langland reaffirms traditional feudal responsibilities as the means to restore order to society, the rebels reaffirm the legitimacy of the feudal order on several occasions. At Saint Albans, for example, the rebels demanded to see the ancient charter of Offa to confirm land boundaries.[11] Caroline M. Barron affirms that the rebels and Langland shared a "simplistic solution to the problems of the realm" in their illusions about an absolutist king who was supposed "to have the support of the common people, to rule in justice, to uphold the laws, to reward his supporters, to defend the church, and to raise money to defend the realm."[12] In addition to their shared ideals, Langland and the rebels shared a position "outside the political nation," and according to Barron therefore "shared a simplistic view of what needed to be done to right the wrongs of the kingdom," which consisted mainly of "the removal of traitors and Lady Meed" from court.[13]

Langland and the rebels also shared a nostalgic vision of the past as a time of order and justice, which helps explain why the rebels found Langland's poem compelling enough to adapt some of its elements for their own purposes. While Langland gives greater credence to church and secular authority, asserting that such institutions can be reformed and that not all their members are necessarily corrupt, the rebels claim to accept only the authority of God, the king, and, occasionally and opportunistically, the authority of ancient documents. But while the rebels appear to have had, like Langland, a fundamentally conservative political vision—including restoring the true church, the king's independence, and the true commons—Langland and the rebels parted in practice; while Langland counseled patient work, the rebels refused to work and wait patiently for the intervention of the king, which would entail waiting for the young monarch not only to come of age, but to cast off his corrupt court. Instead of waiting, the rebels tried to set the restoration in action themselves by freeing the king of evil influences and restoring his place as guarantor of justice; as the Anonimalle chronicler reports, the rebels declared that they had endured "more kings than one" and that they would now "neither suffer nor have any king except King Richard."[14] As steeped in feudal Christian ideology as their targets, the rebels were radical nostalgics; they looked not to the future for a new form of government or social organization, but to the past.

In addressing the ideology of Langland and the rebels, I refer not to a set of beliefs forced upon medieval Christians deliberately in order to subjugate them politically or economically, but to the collective ideas and beliefs of fourteenth-century English society. As Paul Strohm explains, the elements of ideology are "unbound to any one political system" but are instead "unfixed, free-floating, and open to appropriation by contending centers of social power."[15] Strohm notes that because they "are likely to be the property not just of a single social segment but of a society as a whole," the "interpretive schemes" of ideology exhibit a "Janus-faced quality" in which "a single scheme might make a dual appearance, wielded by a chronicler to condemn a rebel action and (rotated on its axis) wielded by the rebels to produce that action in the first place."[16] Whoever interprets the scheme thus harnesses the political and social power of the ideological scheme or element as his own.

One clear illustration of Strohm's assertion is that both the rebels and their targets interpret the events of 1381 in an apocalyptic framework and proclaim their own fellowships as representative of the "true" church in opposition to the company of Antichrist. The ideological struggle between the rebels and their targets is in many ways a hermeneutic battle between those who would interpret their place and the place of their opponents in the apocalyptic paradigm in exactly opposite ways. Who are the "trewemen," and who are the false? Unlike ideological struggles of today, the clash between the established order and the rebels did not focus on which interpretive model should prevail; instead, they fought over control of the terms of the traditional scheme by which they collectively ordered their social history.[17]

From the perspective of the chroniclers and others such as Gower writing from the viewpoint of official culture, the rebellion was a chastisement for sins, and the rebels were one in a series of apocalyptic scourges, as the writer of the short political poem "The Insurrection and the Earthquake" makes clear:

> Þe Rysing of þe comuynes in londe,
> Þe Pestilens, and þe eorþe-quake—
> Þeose þreo þinges, I vnderstonde,
> Beo-tokenes the grete vengaunce & wrake
> Þat schulde falle for synnes sake,
> As this clerkes conne de-clare.
> Nou may we chese to leue or take,
> ffor warnyng haue we to ben ware.[18]

Maintaining that God directly punishes his people for their transgressions and rewards them for their faithfulness and that society endures its final age, the author responded as Langland did to the crises of their time—with calls for reform and apocalyptic warnings. In this inverted world, God allows Antichrist to rule long enough to wreak vengeance as a warning—a "warning to beware" of greater vengeance and Final Judgment.

Walsingham's account of the rebellion in London shows that he too interpreted the events of 1381 according to the apocalyptic model. In his chronicle, Walsingham depicts the uprising as a struggle between the "true

Church" and the forces of Antichrist—in this case, the rebel bands. Walsingham's chronicle characterizes the rebels not only as rustics and animals, but as "doomed ribalds and whores of the devil,"[19] and describes the murder of Sudbury, the "common father of the whole people, the archbishop and primate,"[20] as a martyrdom brought on by the sinfulness of the nation [21] and executed by the "limbs of Satan."[22] From the official point of view represented by Walsingham and other chroniclers, the 1381 Uprising was an attack on the true Church, embodied in the murder of the archbishop, and the rebels actions were anti-Christ. From the perspective of the higher clergy and the nobles, the rebellion demonstrated that Antichrist and his fellows waited just outside the Church and court doors, prepared to topple order and to turn the world upside-down. In this inverted world, according to Walsingham, Sudbury's executioner is punished with blindness for using his sword on the representative of Christ, an anti-miracle that inverts the miracle in which Longinus receives the gift of sight after piercing the side of Jesus with his sword. Immediately following his assurances that God punished the executioner with blindness, Walsingham presents the world righted again by expounding on the miracles that accompanied the archbishop's martyrdom, the first of which is the restoration of sight to a blind man whom the chronicler notes the archbishop had sustained with alms for many years.[23]

Knighton, too, depicts Sudbury and his colleagues as sacrificial victims representative of Christ: "And they, unprotesting and unhesitating, like the lamb before the shearer, their feet bare and their heads uncovered, with their belts loosed, like men taken for murder or robbery and meriting their fate, freely submitted themselves to an undeserved death."[24] Knighton's portrait of the archbishop and treasurer emphasizes that the two voluntarily laid down their lives, a detail clearly not meant to imply that the rebels offered them a choice or to minimize the group's brutality, which Knighton highlights elsewhere; instead, Knighton's depiction of Sudbury and Hales as lambs going to the slaughter like Christ reinforces the identification of the established order as representative of the true society of Christ.

From the rebels' point of view, the world was already upside-down and the Antichrist was already in power, an apocalyptic topos which Langland expresses in agricultural terms:

> Antecrist cam þanne, and al þe crop of truþe
> Torned it tid vp so doun and ouertilte þe roote,
> And made fals sprynge and sprede and spede mennes nedes.

> In ech a contree þer he cam he kutte awey truþe
> And gerte gile growe þere as he a god weere.[25]

In response to just such an inverted world, the rebel task was to turn the world, like Jack Milner's mill, aright. As the surviving rebel messages indicate, the rebels saw themselves and their company as "trewemen" in opposition to traitors to the true Church like Sudbury.[26] While the chroniclers present Sudbury as a Christ figure, for the rebels he is an inversion of Christ—an Antichrist. The Westminster chronicler relates that the rebels produced a grisly display, a parody of the crucifixion with Sudbury's head, on which they had nailed his red cap, hoisted higher than the heads of his fellow victims.[27]

While such a tableau would confirm Sudbury's association with Christ and the true Church in the eyes of those loyal to him, it would sugggest just the opposite to the rebels, as Steven Justice explains:

> The rebel parody mocked the archbishop's pretensions to speak in Christ's name, projecting the image of the crucified Christ . . . as the standard against which he was measured and found wanting. Christ's bloody crown of thorns, symbolic of suffering and authority, was replaced by Sudbury's red cap, symbolic of cardinalatial office and prelatical wealth.[28]

A symbol of the perversion of clerical responsibility and authority, Sudbury is subject to the fury of a crowd that no longer views him as a representative of Christ, but as one who works against the true Church to maintain his wealth and status, a traitor to the Church and to his fellow Christians.

Turning from the rebels' actions to their reported words, we find more evidence that the rebels conceived of their actions as part of the apocalyptic movement of history. Repeating the phrase "now is time," the letters of John Ball and the address of Jack Trewman all rely on the formulaic apocalyptic expression of urgency as a call to fellowship and action.[29] The message of Jack Carter also uses the key phrase, but to a different end, declaring that "nowe is tyme to be ware."[30]

Whether Knighton's description of the gathering of rebels and their speeches is an historically accurate representation or Knighton's own synthesis of rebel materials, the order of the messages is more significant than usually admitted; in fact, the order in which the messages appear in Knighton's chronicle not only strongly suggests that Knighton synthesized his sources, but provides important clues to understanding the production and goals of the rebel messages.

After Knighton introduces the rebel leaders as Thomas Baker, Jack Straw, Jack Milner, Jack Carter, and Jack Trewman, he reports, "Jakke Mylner alloquitur socios sic," suggesting that the messages that follow were speeches directed to the assembled crowd of 20,000. A closer reading of the texts, however, suggests that they were composed in different stages of the rebellion: Milner's message calls for fellowship; Carter's message urges preparation for the revolt and warns of treachery; and Trewman's message is a final call to action. If, as I believe, the rebel messages are not only from different, but successive stages of the rebellion, we can conclude that Knighton compiled the communications, most likely from written scraps like the copy of John Ball's letter to the Essex commons which Walsingham reports was found in the tunic of a man about to be hanged for his part in the revolt.[31] And while Knighton did not recognize the probable time lapse between the rebel "speeches" and therefore compressed the time before the revolt into one meeting of leaders and rebels, his hindsight and skill as a reader and chronicler may have steered him to arrange the messages in chronological order from the call for support, to the preparatory warning, to the urgent call for justice. One other possibility, of course, is that certain rebels in the course of their reported celebrating recited the successive messages to their bands as a sort of rebel performance or proclamation, a summary and celebration of their planning and action. In either case, these messages figure the revolt according to the apocalyptic model, as a dualistic battle of suppressed good against the rule of evil.

In the first of Knighton's reported communications, Milner calls for fellowship and asks for help to right his mill, a fitting image for revolutionary action that also recalls the wheel of fortune. Milner's message employs apocalyptic phrases and economic metaphors to suggest ethical boundaries within which the rebels could turn the mill aright, even if that effort necessitated violence, and to underscore both the misrule of the powerful and their imminent fall. Employing the apocalyptic motif of the world upside down during the period when Antichrist and his forces thrive, Milner promises that Christ will mete out justice in terms that both reflect the economic metaphors of salvation history and underscore the economic motives for the rebellion:

> Iakke Mylner asket help to turne hys mylne aright. He hath gronden smal smal, þe kyngus sone of heuen he schal pay for alle. Loke þi mylne go aryȝt, wiþ þe foure sayles, and þe post stande in stedefastnesse. Wiþ ryȝt & with myȝt, wiþ skyl and wiþ wylle, lat myȝt helpe ryȝt, and skyl go before wille, and ryȝt before myȝt, þan goth

> oure mylne aryght, and if myȝt go before ryght, and wylle before skylle, þan is oure mylne mys a dyȝt.[32]

The allegorical mill, with its four sails of right, might, skill and will—respectively, justice, power, the ability to discriminate what is proper, and desire or volition—is an allegory of both economic and political action; the description of the mill's correct operation thus advances an ethical model not only for proper economic interaction, but for the revolt. When the mill runs correctly—when might helps right, when discretion supersedes desire, and when right supersedes might—the post is upright and steadfast and Jack gets to grind his corn. By recalling the violence of the harvest in apocalyptic lore and by deferring to Christ's judgment in the chiliastic assertion that follows, that "þe kyngus sone of heuen he schal pay for alle," the message of Milner employs the apocalyptic imagery of the thresher and winepress to suggest that those who had perverted the mill had earned their violent fate. Likewise, the message's conclusion that the mill is "mys adyȝt" when might goes before right and desire goes before discretion has, as Steven Justice notes, "an obvious relevance to the public justification, and self-justification, of revolutionary violence."[33] Asserting that they act on the side of truth to return the world to its proper order, the rebels figuratively act as an arm of Christ, which would allow them to condone violence as righteous punishment and as a means to set the mill and society aright.

The matters of who runs the mill and whether it is run properly are not just figurative, but practical concerns. The mill is not just an allegory of economic power and action, but a concrete example that embodies the sort of economic struggles that propelled the revolt. The control of milling rights, fees, and profits was central to the commons' economic struggle and survival in the face of manorial and monastic control and corruption. The ideological and economic power of milling is clear from the struggle over milling rights between the commons and the monks of the manor at St. Albans. Demanding the right to use handmills, the rebels gouged the floor of the cloister to reclaim the handmills with which the floor had been paved, brought out the pieces, and distributed them to the rest of the commons outside in a manner Walsingham likens to the sharing of the eucharist.[34]

With the feast of Corpus Christi just two days before the handmill incident at St. Albans, Walsingham's observations could reflect his own religious orientation or record the purposeful communion of the rebels, inspired to enact a eucharist not of bread, but of the means to produce their own bread.[35] The latter seems most likely, as Walsingham usually characterizes the rebels as uncontrollable brutes unless their actions compel him otherwise, as did the rebel ban against looting at the Savoy. As a "source of [the rising's] public idiom,"[36] in the words of Justice, the feast of Corpus Christi celebrated not only the physical body of Christ, but the mystical body that is Christ's Church,[37] the community of believers. Seizing the symbolic means to produce bread, including eucharistic bread, the rebels celebrated their place as members of the True Church and therefore as limbs of Christ's True Church, a designation in the apocalyptic context that serves to justify violence against one's oppressors.

Knighton's second rebel message, the address of Jack Carter, was apparently composed later than the message of Milner. Following Milner's call for fellowship, Carter's communication addresses conspirators preparing for the revolt, urging them to continue preparations warily to ensure their success:

> Iakke Cart*er* preyes ȝowe alle, þat ȝe make a gode ende of þat ȝe haue begunnen, and doþ wele and ay bettur and bettur, for at þe euen men heryth þe day. For if þe ende be wele, þan is alle wele. Lat Peres þe Plowman my broþur duelle at home and dyȝt vs corne, and I wil go wiþ ȝowe and helpe þat y may to dyȝte ȝoure mete and ȝoure drynke, þ*at* ȝe none fayle. Lokke þat Hobbe robbyoure be wele chastysede for lesyng of ȝoure g*ra*ce, for ȝe have gret nede to take god wiþ ȝowe in alle ȝoure dedes. For nowe is tyme to be ware.[38]

Enlisting Langland's ideal figure of the true commons, Carter proclaims Piers the Plowman his brother, and thus a fellow of the rebels' company. In naming "Peres þe Plowman my broþur" as part of his company, Carter appropriates Langland's figure of the true working Christian for rebel purposes. Adopting Langland's dualistic scheme of the honest husbandman and the robber Hobbe, the message of Carter applies the apocalyptic dichotomy to contemporary circumstance; describing the attack on Hobbe as chastisement, the rebels act as the arm of Christ striking down the enemies of Piers and his fellows, the true Church. Bolstering this justification of violence is Carter's assertion that "if þe ende be wele, þan is alle wele," which not only asserts that the end justifies the means, but reassures the rebels that if they are successful in overthrowing their powerful persecutors, they will not have to fear punishment themselves. Still, the fear underlying Carter's message is palpable on its conclusion, "For nowe is tyme to be ware," which calls to mind both careful defense and material preparedness.

Similar to the letter of John Ball that Walsingham reports was found in the clothing of a man about to be executed, Carter's message not only enlists Langland's symbol of Christian perfection, Piers, but reiterates and redefines the terminology of *Piers Plowman's* salvific scheme. The rebel messages transform *dowel*, *dobet*, and *dobest* into codewords for various stages of their efforts, the same stages reflected in Knighton's chronology of the rebel messages. Redefining the key terms of Langland's scheme, the rebels transform terms that in *Piers Plowman* refer to the progressive and cumulative steps necessary for individual and social perfection into terms that designate stages of rebel involvement. Broadly speaking, in *Piers Plowman* to *dowel* is to accept Christian belief and fellowship; to *dobet* is to engage in right action to prepare one's soul, such as giving to the poor; and to *dobest* is to oppose evil actively for the sake of others. For the rebels, to *dowel* was to respond to the call of fellowship, to ally oneself with the true commons in their struggle; to *dobet* was to take preliminary action to prepare for the struggle, often expressed in terms of producing and readying supplies such as food and drink; and to *dobest* was to engage finally in the struggle, to chastise those who oppose the true commons and Church. From this frame of reference, Carter's admonition to do well and "ay bettur and bettur" urges conspirators to continue preparations already underway.

The final rebel "speech" in Knighton's chronicle reiterates Milner's claim that the world is upside down and calls for the revolt to begin. Asserting that false sinners have overcome the true flock, Jack Trewman's message is a call from the true commons to all true people to help restore the proper order of society:

> Iakke Trewman doþ ȝow to understande þat falsnes and gyle haviþ regned to longe, & trewþe hat bene sette under a lokke, and falnes regneth in euerylk flokke. No man may come trewþe to, but he syng si dedero. Speke spend and spede, quoth Ion of Banthon, and þ*er*fore synne fareth as wylde flode, trew loue is away, þat was so gode, and clerkus for welthe worche hem wo. God do bote, for / nowȝe is tyme.[39]

No longer referring to the "tyme to be ware" as does the conclusion of Carter's message, but identifying the time to act, the last words of Trewman, "God do bote, for nowȝe is tyme," urge social action in typically apocalyptic terms.

By framing the imminent revolt as a great battle between persons true and false, between true Christians and traitors to the true faith and the community, Trewman's message relies on both apocalyptic urgency and dualism for motivating and justifying actions meant to turn the evil world aright. In this sense, Trewman's address reasserts the rebel ethics Milner's message sets forth. As the ethical tie that binds, as a "standard of behavior" as Steven Justice describes it in a discussion of one of John Ball's letters, *trewþe* not only indicates rightness of thought and action, but "describes a relation (standing 'togedyr') that makes *trewþe* a normative concept to which the rebels can appeal and which also indicates the presence of divine grace."[40] Expecting God's help as long as he and his allies act on the behalf of Truth, Trewman calls for justice to restore "trewe loue" in a society in which bribery silences the truth and undermines justice. By identifying *trewþe*, the binding tie of feudal society, as the basis of rebel fellowship, Trewman's message reveals the traditional nature of rebel ideology.

Of the same character, language, and, some would argue, the same author as the addresses of Milner, Carter, and Trewman,[41] the letters of John Ball also abound with apocalyptic commonplaces, and once again, the messages' allusions to *Piers Plowman* appear key to their meaning, even if that meaning is not wholly decipherable. And just as Knighton records the addresses of Milner, Carter and Trewman in their probable chronological order, we can infer a rough chronological order for John Ball's letters by comparing his use of the structure and language of *Piers Plowman* to that of the other rebel messages.

Closest in language, imagery, and probably time of composition are the messages of Carter and the letter of John Ball to the commons of Esssex that Walsingham reports was found at a rebel execution. Warning conspirators to lay low and beware treachery, Ball stresses the need for fellowship and solidarity:

> Johon schep som tyme seynte marie prest of ȝork. and now of colchestre. Greteth wel johan nameles and joh*a*n þe mullere and johon carter and biddeþ hem þat þei bee war of gyle in borugh and stondeþ [togidere] in godes name. and biddeþ Peres plouȝman. go to his werk. and chastise wel hobbe þe robbere. and takeþ wiþ ȝow joh*a*n trewman and alle hijs felawes and no mo. and loke schappe ȝou to on heued and no mo. joh*a*n þe mullere haþ ygrounde smal smal smal þe kynges sone of heuene schal paye for al. be war or [ȝ]e be wo knoweþ ȝour frend fro ȝour foo. haueth ynow. & seith hoo. and do wel and bettre and fleth synne. and sekeþ pees and hold ȝou þer inne. and so biddeþ joh*a*n trewaman and alle his felawes.[42]

Like the address of Carter, Ball's letter suggests that at the time of its composition, preparations for the revolt were already underway. Like Carter, Ball adapts Langland's salvific scheme to indicate phases of rebel action, but he restricts Carter's urging "doþ ay bettur and bettur" by adding a moral injunction urging restraint, "haueth ynow. & seith hoo. and do wel and bettre and fleth synne," a fitting warning for a cleric which shows us that Ball not only believed that the impending revolt was justified and righteous, but that the rebel aims could be accomplished within moral and ethical bounds. At the same time, Ball's warning here against sin and his advice "loke schappe ȝou to on heued and no mo" urges leadership, organization and focus in the face of what could, and clearly at times did, degenerate into an uncontrollable mob.

Like the addresses of Milner, Carter and Trewman, Ball cleaves society into two opposing forces: the fellows of the Trewman, including Piers Plowman, John Miller, John Carter, and John Nameless; and their foes, the fellows of Hobbe the robber. The figural and pseudonymous character of the rebel names tells us much about how Ball and the rebel conspirators imagined and organized themselves. All bearing the name John except for Piers the plowman, a sign not only of solidarity but of the necessary anonymity suggested by "John Nameless," the rebel leaders whom Ball lists represent the primary occupations of rural economic life. Those who plow, mill, and cart, all "true men" or true commons, share the same enemies and fellows, so that in addition to working as pseudonyms for various rebel leaders with different functions in the revolt, the names Ball lists imply a metonomy between the rebel leaders and their followers, the others who perform various functions in the uprising: Piers lays the seeds or the groundwork for the revolt and works directly to chastise Hobbe; Miller and his fellows process the harvest, grinding down their enemies to secure justice according to the popular apocalyptic motif; and Carter goes with them, helping to transport goods and people during the revolt.

The first names of the rebels whom Ball addresses, the names of the writer of the Apocalypse and of the first leader of the Church, identify the rebels as acting on the side of, and in the name of, the true Church. Furthermore, with his warning of danger, admonition to beware of enemies in town, and appeal for the company to stand together and finish what they had begun, Ball recalls the apostles and early Church beseiged. When the rebels in Knighton's chronicle name themselves, they use the nickname Jack, a more informal, rural appellation appropriate for their status that suggests an occupational solidarity separate from the spiritual and moral solidarity the cleric Ball implies.

While the John Ball letter in Walsingham gives direction for the same stage in the preparation and execution of the revolt as does the message of Carter, one of the other two John Ball letters reported by Knighton calls directly for action and can thus be dated nearer the revolt than Ball's other letters. Like the message of Trewman, both of the letters Knighton records use the apocalyptic commonplace "the time is now," although to different ends.

This first message recorded by Walsingham, the *Examplar*, uses the phrase "Nowe is tyme" in the same way Trewman does, as a call to set the revolt in motion, to finish what the rebel conspirators had begun:

> Exemplar epistole Iohannis Balle.
>
> Ion Balle gretyþ ȝow wele alle & doþ ȝowe to understande, he haþ rungen ȝoure belle. Nowe ryȝt & myȝt, wylle and skylle. God spede every y dele. Nowe is tyme lady helpe to Iesu þi sone, and þi sone to his fadur, to mak a gode ende, in þe name of þe Trinite, of þat is be gunne. Amen, Amen, pur charite, Amen.[43]

Preceding his reference to the key terms set forth in Milner's allegory of the mill—ryȝt and myȝt, wylle and skylle—with the word "nowe," Ball prays for help so that the rebels might succeed and make a "gode ende" of what they had begun. Ball's repetitious prayer closing the letter smacks of fervent prayer just before a battle.

The second letter above, which Knighton designates as the "first letter" of John Ball, uses the phrase "now is the time" in a similar way to the message of Milner:

> Prima epistola Iohannis Balle.
>
> Iohan Balle, Seynte Marye prist greėȝ wele alle maner men and byddes hem in þe name of þe trinite, faddur, and sone and holy gost, stonde manlyche togedyr in trewþe, and helpeȝ trewþe, and trewþe schal helpe ȝowe. Nowe regneþ pride in pris, and couetys is hold wys, and leccherye wiþ[outen shame] and glotonye wiþ outen blame. Enuye regniþ wiþ tresone, and slouthe is take in grete sesone. God do bote, for nowe is tyme. Amen.[44]

Like Milner's address, this letter calls for fellowship and justifies that call in the apocalyptic framework. Ball's use of the phrase "for nowe is tyme" here thus refers not to the outbreak of the revolt, but to the call for fellowship at the beginning of letter and to the rhyme that follows, which asserts the contemporary reign of the deadly sins—the same appocalyptic motif of the world inverted that Milner presents in the allegory of the mill. And just as Milner assures the rebels that "þe kyngus sone of heuen he schal pay for alle," Ball urges unity and anticipates success because he expects God's help in a righteous cause. Instructing the rebels, "stonde manlyche togedyr in trewþe, and helpeȝ trewþe, and trewþe schal helpe ȝowe,"[45] Ball moves from an abstract definition of truth to a proper noun; as Steven Justice notes, the movement of "truth" from adverb to object to noun here "seems to have achieved the theological sense" we find in *Piers Plowman*: "God will help you."[46]

Another indication of the apocalyptic underpinnings of John Ball's language and imagery is clear when we examine his transformation of a commonplace poem on the deadly sins:

Ball:	Index, No. 2356:[47]
Nowe regneþ pride in pris	Now pride ys yn pris,
and couetys is hold wys	Now couetyse ys wyse,
and lecherye wiþouten shame	Now lechery ys schameles,
and glotonye withouten blame	Now gloteny ys lawles,
Enuye regniþ wiþ tresone	Now slewþe ys yn seson,
and slouthe is take in grete sesone	In envie & wreþe ys treson;
god do bote. for nowe is tyme	Now haþ god enchesyn
amen	to dystrie þys worle by reson [48]

Here Ball transforms, in the words of Rossell Hope Robbins, a "typical complaint, which could be found in the books or on the lips of any orthodox cleric or layman" into a "call for action."[49] If Ball knew the rhyme in a form similar to the one above, as their parallels suggest, he altered its ending, replacing the original apocalyptic expression promising destruction with another phrase more chiliastic and millenarian in character. Praying for God's help and stressing the nearness of the battle, Ball downplays the potential destruction and violence of the uprising. Omitting the rhyme's reference in the final lines to God's destruction of the world, Ball skirts the question of possible disaster. Ball's uncoupling of envy and wrath removes any suggestion that the rebels act out of sinful motives, and by shifting the sin of envy from one committed by treasonous subjects to their leaders, those who "reign," Ball asserts the treasonous behavior of those in power and underscores the righteousness of the rebel cause. Similarly, by omitting wrath from the list of deadly sins, a fact no doubt noted by his audience, Ball implies that rebel anger is not sinful, but righteous.

In each discussion of rebel actions and texts above, I have attempted to show what, why, and how some of the 1381 rebels communicated. Implicit in this attempt is my assumption that Ball's letters and the other rebel messages are indeed messages—that they convey information and encouragement that undermine any suggestion by the chroniclers that the rebels had neither the ability nor the sophistication to act in concert. Judging from the crowd's refusal to loot the Savoy, Walsingham's description of the rebels at St. Albans, the size and various locations of the uprising, and the very presence of the cryptic rebel letters, we must admit the rebels had at least rudimentary, and perhaps fairly sophisticated, means of communication. That the uprising at times was no more than an uncontrollable and brutal mob scene does nothing to repudiate this idea, given what often happens to best laid plans and how easily group action degenerates into rioting. The fact that the revolt became as violent and as widespread as it did suggests less a lack of coordination than the power of rebel ideas and the extent to which those ideas touched a nerve in the population.

In the discussion above, I have also presumed that John Ball did not author all six messages, a point on which scholars are divided. R. B. Dobson assumes all six texts are Ball's;[50] Hilton calls attention to the rebel pseudonyms as names "possibly for Ball himself";[51] and Green hesitantly agrees with Dobson.[52] More probable, I believe, is the scenario Stephen Justice describes, in which the reiteration of rebel messages resulted in various textual mutations that suggest not a common author, nor independent production, but "an initial body of such letters [that] incited a pattern of imitation, recombination, and distribution."[53] Although he initially dismisses the question of authorship as "umpromising: quaintly empirical and in any case insoluble,"[54] he later suggests that Ball's letters set off a "epistolary practice" among the rebels, an assertion he supports with a statement from the *Anonimalle Chronicle*: "The commons sent several letters to Kent, Suffolk and Norfolk [urging them] to rise along with themselves."[55] Further supporting multiple authorhip, I believe, is the fact that it would make no sense for Ball to give instructions, if coded ones, to the rebels "johan þe mullere," "johon carter," and "johan trewman" if these were his own pseudonyms.

The obvious conclusion to be drawn here is that, if John Ball did not author all the rebel messages, other conspirators were able to employ the "dark" language necessary to communicate rebel information covertly; another obvious conclusion is that a number of their cohorts could read, or at least interpret, such messages.

Like Robbins and G. R. Owst before him, Green successfully demonstrates that the six rebel texts "reflect the world of the popular preacher, their proverbs and scraps of vernacular verse turning up in sermons, sermon notes, and preaching manuals throughout the fourteenth century,"[56] but because he begins with the assumption that John Ball wrote all six, Green concludes that his search for sources "seems to have taught us little more than we knew already."[57] But if, as I believe, John Ball did not write all six, a study like Green's has much to teach us about rebel reading and writing, hermeneutics and imitation, for the gener-ation of rebel texts then indicates a wide currency of typical representation and commonplace expressions that the rebels manipulated to produce subversive and secret messages. Whether John Ball authored all six texts or not, others had to be able to interpret them, and because popular preachers used such commonplaces, not only they but their listeners must have been familiar with such material.

John Ball and his fellows consistently constructed messages obscure enough to convey a conservative message to some while conveying radical information to others by choosing traditional material that could convey both traditional and radical sentiments at once. The doubleness of this language, the masking of rebel messages with traditional turns of phrase, produces two sorts of possible readings for the rebel messages—one profoundly conservative, the other clearly rebellious. In fact, any reading today of these texts must beg the question of intent; because we know so little about the circumstances of production and the immediate audience of these writings, we either assume that they are the products of conservative thinkers and thus convey a traditional message, or we assume that the authors were conveying messages about the revolt and thus produce a radical reading.

What is important here is that both sorts of readings these texts elicit from contemporaries and critics alike were necessary for the rebel communications to be effective—i.e., to relay information to select persons and to remain opaque, conventional expressions for those who do not or cannot interpret the texts' code. For example, when Carter states "i wil go wiþ ȝowe and helpe þat y may to dyȝte ȝoure mete and ȝoure drynke þat ȝe none fayle," one might conclude that Carter will help transport food and drink to sustain the population, which reflects his typical occupation. For someone planning a rebellion, however, the phrase "þat ȝe none fayle" takes on a whole new meaning; Carter's working "so that you do not fail" then refers not to the failure of individuals' bodies, but to the failure of the rebel body. Masking a statement about preparations for the revolt with a harmless and obvious statement about sustenance and victualling, Carter's message implies that the rebels must act as a unified body if they wish to chastise Hobbe. The last words of Carter's message, "ffor nowe is tyme to be ware," display another double message. On the surface is a typical warning no more subversive than the one tendered in "The Insurrection and the Earthquake," while the deeper reading simultaneously urges caution and continuing preparation for a revolt, for "to be ware" is both to beware of betrayal and to be prepared, to be busy supplying the necessary wares for the uprising. The phrase "to be ware" also restricts the call to action "nowe is tyme," and thus sets the time for wary preparation in contrast with the time for active revolt. In another instance of a seemingly commonplace expression concealing the instruction for provisioning, Carter reminds the rebels, "[ȝe] haue gret nede to take god wiþ ȝowe in alle ȝoure dedes," which appears a harmless reminder about the need for God and good deeds. If, however, one reads "goods" for "god," one finds another statement about the importance of supplying provisions for the revolt.

Because the rebel messages use traditional and common phrases to subversive ends, a false dilemma in scholarship on the letters has persisted which has caused critics to divide into two camps. While some critics focus on the political and subversive character of such texts, another group minimizes the political or revolutionary content of the letters because they have characteristics of traditional genres such as estates satire. Green tentatively reconciles both views, represented by Rossell Hope Robbins and George Kane:

> There is after all the possibility that Ball's letters are indeeed entirely conventional, but that for some reason their very conventions, however pacific in origin, had become inflammatory by 1381. Traditional complaint literature may well have been as profoundly conservative in outlook as Kane claims, but if at the same time it helped articulate and focus popular discontent, as Robbins suggests, perhaps this was because those who rallied to its call were also conservative—because they were trying to prevent a new age, not usher one in.[58]

With the goals of restoring an ideal feudal society, of "trying to prevent a new age," the rebels relied on traditional values such as *trewþe* and traditional language of reform, and that such expressions were conventional does not mean that they were not subversive, as Kane suggests, but that such expressions could be subversive without the rebels' enemies recognizing them as such.

Kane's own reading of parts of two of John Ball's letters provides a fine example of the sort of reading that the rebels may have wished their contemporary opponents would produce upon discovering such communications—one that reveals nothing about rebel plans:

> As for the revolutionary implications of Ball's two 'letters', they have been exaggerated. One actually admonishes against precipitous action: *be war or ye be wo*, 'be cautious before your bring unhappiness upon yourselves', and *haueth ynow*

> *and seith hoo!*, 'When you have a sufficiency, say "Stop"'. 'Flee sin', it proposes, 'seek peace, keep yourselves in peace'. The other is in effect a complaint about the prevalence of six of the seven capital sins (the absent one is, significantly, anger) followed by prayer, *God doe boote for nowe is tyme*, 'May God effect a remedy, for the moment has come.'[59]

This sort of reading is just what anyone who constructs a coded message hopes that text can produce when taken at face value: innocuous statements in which subversive meaning lies unnoticed on the table like Poe's purloined letter. Alternately, "be war or ȝe be wo knoweþ ȝour frend fro ȝour foo, haueth ynow. & seith hoo" urges not inaction and complacency while waiting for God's justice, but cautious preparation and wariness in choosing fellows: "Beware and be prepared or be sorry; be cautious and do not admit your enemies into your fellowship; limit the number of people who know your plans, and do not act immoderately."

In each of the readings above I have attempted, in the words of Richard Firth Green, "the picking of textual locks"[60] by examining rebel actions, texts, and subtexts—most notably, *Piers Plowman*—in the context of apocalyptic culture. The propensity that the rebel messages exhibit for double and concealed messages helps explain how rebels familiar with *Piers Plowman* responded to the poem and why they found it useful in attracting support for their cause. Like the rebel messages, *Piers Plowman* relies on puns and multiple meanings to suggest more than is obvious on the surface of the text.[61] Furthermore, a reader looking for hidden meanings and messages to support his cause could twist fairly conventional episodes from *Piers Plowman* to support rebel action. For example, preparing for the assault of the forces of Antichrist in Passus XX, Conscience calls the people of Christ into Unity:

> 'I conseille', quod Conscience þo, 'comeþ wiþ me, ye fooles,
> Into vnite holy chirche and holde we vs þere.
> And crye we to kynde þat he come and defende vs
> Fooles fro þise fendes lymes, for Piers loue þe Plowman.
> And crye we on al þe comune þat þei come to vnitee
> And þere abide and bikere ayeins Beliales children.'[62]

Several details of this short passage alone show the appeal of Langland's poem for rebel leaders; the passage's call to unity, identification of the company of Piers as those defending themselves against the company of the devil, and suggestion that those who answer the call of conscience are both holy fools and fools in the eyes of Antichrist's corrupt society all reinforce key features of the rebels' apocalyptic identity. Given their chosen role in the apocalyptic model, the rebels who believed they acted in the name of God by chastising those who would harm God's people imagined themselves working on the side of Piers Plowman.

CONCLUSION

Plowmen After Piers

The influence of *Piers Plowman* is clear from the poems of Langland's imitators, for whom the figure of the plowman as the true Christian working for not only the sustenance but the salvation of others continues to represent the plight of the commons pressured by corrupt lords and clerics. And although the later poems do not all exhibit the apocalyptic urgency or millenarian hopes of Langland's poem, they all adopt the dualistic framework of apocalyptic history along with various elements of Langland's poem to characterize their opponents and targets as anti-Christ, as the kin of Cain and the devil. Rather than announce the need for comprehensive social renovation as Langland does, his imitators satirize the clergy and nobles, often pointing out their corruption cynically and with little expectation of change.

In *Pierce* [or *Peres*] *the Ploughman's Crede*, a wanderer sets out in search of someone to teach him his creed, but has no success with any order of friars, who consistently exhibit one or more of the seven deadly sins and who are all eager to absolve the wanderer for a fee, telling him not to bother learning his Creed. A fine example of clerical satire in the service of Wycliffite sentiments, the poem contrasts the worldly motives and unethical behavior of all four orders of friars with the ideal behavior of the poor but charitable plowman and the saints who founded the friars' orders. After describing the infiltration of the "wilde wer-wolves,"[1] man-wolves in the sheep's clothing of their pastoral duties, the poet contrasts these fiends who destroy the faith with the founders and rules of their orders:

> Þei don nouȝt after Domynick but dreccheþ þe puple,
> Ne folwen nouȝt Fraunces but falslyche lybben,

And Austynes rewle þei rekneþ but a fable,
But purchaseþ hem pryuylege of popes at Rome.[2]

Rather than following the founders and rules of their orders, first a Franciscan, then a Dominican, Augustinian, and Carmelite offer the wanderer absolution for payment. In each case, the friar enacts an important part of the final passus of the B-text of *Piers Plowman*: the infiltration of Holy Church by antichrist friars who absolve the sinner for their own profit, with no attention to the demands of Conscience. Like the antichrist friar who does not act as Christ the Physician in *Piers Plowman*, but instead tricks Conscience, all the friars of *Peres the Ploughmans Crede* are willing to absolve the sinner and let him go "wiþouten any peine"[3] and with only a promise to return with money or goods, "Wiþ som katell oþer corne or cuppes of siluer."[4] By not applying a properly painful plaster, which in Langland's poem represents the healing power of proper penance, the friars betray their sacramental duties and endanger those whose souls they should save.

While the wanderer, weeping like Langland's Will, can find no friar to help him, he comes upon a pathetic plowman and his family, who offer him solace and sustenance as best they can. While the friars unctiously try to win the wanderer into supporting them by calling him son, "felawe," and "leue leel man,"[5] only the plowman ankle deep in mud—with his wife barefoot and bleeding on the ice, crying twins, and baby in rags in an old bowl—offers the wanderer true brotherhood: "ȝif þe lakke lijflode lene þe ich will / Swich good as God haþ sent go we, leue broþer."[6] This plowman, who later identifies himself as "Peres . . . þe pore man þe ploweman"[7] is no simple peasant, but a discerning Christian who, despite his poverty and hardships, recognizes greedy and proud members of the clergy as "false profetes in þe feiþ"[8] who do the work of the devil. Peres echoes his namesake in characterizing the corrupt clergy as wolves in sheep's clothing. Quoting Matthew 7:15, Peres reveals his knowledge of scripture:

'*In vestimentis ouium* but onlie wiþ-inne
Þei ben wilde wer-wolues þat wiln þe folk robben.'
Þe fend founded hem, first þe feiþ to destroie,
And by his craft þei comen in to combren þe chirche.[9]

These clerics are not the poor preachers Christ ordained, but are "of Kaymes kynde."[10] Criticizing able-bodied, well-dressed and adequately fed clerics who beg,[11] Peres echoes his predecessor in Langland's poem, where Piers scolds able-bodied beggars who refuse to work in Passus VI and calls them "wastours."[12]

Like Langland, the poet criticizes friars who ally themselves with rich lords instead of the poor. In a display of pride and anger, an Austin friar in *Pierce the Plowmans Crede* criticizes the Minorites, or Franciscans:

> Lordes loueth hem well for þei so lowe crouchen;
> But knewen men her cautel & her queynt wordes,
> Þei wolde worchypen hem nouȝt but a litel,
> Þe image of ypocricie ymped vpon fendes.[13]

Himself a hypocrite, the Austin friar then offers the wanderer absolution, but only with a promise of material compensation.[14] The wary wanderer, however, sees through the friar's sinful motive and declares, "Heere pride is þe pater-noster . . . / Heere Crede is coveytise."[15]

The wanderer of *Peres the Ploughmans Crede*, like his predecessor in Langland's poem, hopes to find a moral authority he cannot find in the corrupt clergy, and the plowman represents that authority in both poems. In the later poem, however, the plowman is not a mystical conflation of Christ, Peter, and every true working Christian, but a ragged laborer who symbolizes the moral superiority of the commons in the face of contemporary corruption. The protagonist of *Peres the Ploughmans Crede* does not assume that he will find moral or spiritual authority only among the clergy; as he sets out to learn his Creed, the wanderer promises to search for a proper teacher whether learned or not:

> Þerfor lerne þe byleue leuest me were,
> And if any werkly wiȝt wille me couþe,
> Oþer lewed or lered þat lyueþ þer after,
> And fulliche folweth þe feyþ and feyneþ non oþer.[16]

"Knowing" one's creed well enough to teach it here does not indicate mere book knowledge, but knowing how to follow Christ by rejecting worldly goods and goals. The wanderer seeks a Christian who is not attracted by the wealth of this world:

> Þat no worldliche wele wilneþ no tyme,
> But lyueþ in louynge of God and his lawe holdeþ,

And for no getynge of good neuuer his God greueþ,
But followeþ him þe full wey as he þe folke taughte.[17]

To follow Christ the "full way"—i.e., in both word and deed—is to live in poverty. When he meets Peres, the wanderer is lamenting, "y can fynden no man þat fully byleueþ / To techen me þe heyȝe weie," which clearly links his quest with the work of Langland's plowman, who waits to go on pilgrimage because he has "an half acre to erie by þe heiȝe weye."[18] In Passus X of *Piers Plowman*, Study identifies the "high way" as the road to clergy, but adds that he who wishes to arrive must ride by riches and be ready to endure both weal and woe.[19] The work Piers does when he plows the half acre is thus not strictly agricultural labor, but the work of the Church, and all clergy who wish to take the "high way" must do the work their vocation asks in voluntary poverty.

By juxtaposing religious ideals with real signs of contemporary clerical corruption, the poet adapts Langland's distinction between true and false treasure, between spiritual and material wealth, to underscore just how spiritually bankrupt the wealthy friars are. In some of the most pointed satire of the poem, the Franciscan discusses the sort of life his order's founder advocated:

We hauen forsaken the worlde & in wo lybbeþ,
In penaunce & pouerte & precheþ þe puple,
By ensample of oure life soules to helpen;
And in pouertie praien for all oure parteners
Þat ȝyueþ vs any good god to honouren,
Oþer bell oþer booke or breed to our fode,
Oþer catell oþer cloþ to coueren wiþ our bones,
Money or money-worthe; here mede is in heven.[20]

Setting clerical ideals against contemporary practices, the poet satirizes his targets and underscores their corruption. The friar then describes the convent, church, and chapel he and his brethren hope to build, showing clearly that they are storing up their treasure here on earth instead of in heaven. First urging the wanderer to contribute for his spiritual benefit, the friar reveals his assumption that potential contributors are sinfully proud and fond of ostentation when he later tries to peddle a place on a stained-glass window:

And myȝtestou amenden vs wiþ money of þyn owne,
Þou chuldest cnely bifore Crist in compas of gold

In the wide windowe westwarde wel niȝe in the myddell,
And seynt Fraunces himself schall folden the in his cope,
And presente the to the trynite and praie for thy synnes.
Þi name schall noblich ben wryten & wrouȝt for the nones,
And, in remembrance of þe, yrade þer for euer.[21]

Confusing spiritual wealth and brotherhood with signs of material wealth and pride and replacing the protection and spiritual brotherhood of Saint Francis with a scene of "gaie glittering glas glowing as þe sonne,"[22] the friar undermines Church by seducing sinners into committing the deadly sin of pride. Instead of being written forever in the Book of the Living, the names of contributors are written "forever" on windows of glass, a fitting contrast of spiritual surety with materialistic fragility. When the wanderer comes upon the Dominican minster, he sees the sort of display the Franciscan recommends, mainly funded by merchants:

Wyde wyndows y-wrouȝt y-written full þikke,
Schynen wiþ schapen scheldes to schewen aboute,
Wiþ merkes of merchauntes ymedled bytwene,
Mo þan twenty and two twyes ynoumbred.
Þer is none heraud þat haþ halt swich a rolle,
Riȝt as a rageman haþ rekned hem newe.[23]

These merchants on the ragman's roll, by definition a legal list, have been "reckoned"—both judged and counted—on the devil's roll, a list of the damned that is the opposite of God's Book of the Living. As in *Piers Plowman*, in which Piers beats the ragman with a pole to steal back fruit, or souls,[24] this poet classifies those who try to buy and sell forgiveness as the damned fellowship of the devil. After admiring the stained glass windows, the wanderer describes alabaster and marble "Tombes opon tabernacles" of rich lords and ladies, which underscores the futility of storing earthly treasure, the inevitability of death, and the judgment that will surely follow.

The poet of *Peres the Plowmans Crede* consistently juxtaposes the wasteful expenditures of clerics and the rich with the poverty and taxes of the commons. The wanderer comments on the tombs described above, measuring their cost in terms of tax collections: "Þouȝ þe tax of ten ȝer were trewly y-gadered, / Nolde it nouȝt maken þat hous half, as y trowe."[25] Again showing the practical consequences of sinful extravagance, the poet comments on the value of a painted and polished pillar in the Dominicans' convent: "Þe pris of a plouȝ-lond of penyes so rounde / To aparaile þat pyler were pure lytel."[26] After more than fifty lines describing the Dominicans' luxurious accommodations, the narrator points out the hypocrisy of wealthy clerics who beg and asserts that such extravagant lifestyles are at the expense of the poor: "And ȝet þise bilderes wilne beggen a baggful of wheate / Of a pore man þat maie oneþe paie / Half his rente in a ȝer and half ben behynde!"[27] Like the confessor friar in Passus III of *Piers Plowman* who proclaims, "I shal assoille þee myself for a seem of whete" and then asks for the shirt off a man's back,[28] these friars are not in the service of Holy Church, but of Falsehood; they are the company of Antichrist. Just as Langland did, this poet asserts that the means to salvation is proper work and that the way to earn damnation is by wasting or refusing to do one's proper work.

Like Langland, the poet of *Peres the Ploughmans Crede* reaffirms traditional social divisions. Echoing Langland, who complains about those with only rudimentary educations becoming priests, Peres rejects the children of cobblers who become bishops and to whom lords' sons then bow as an affront to the dignity of the bishop's office and to those of "gentil blod"; however, Peres's derision toward the poor men's children and toward the cobbler when he complains about the deference of knights to such clerics seems inappropriate from the mouth of a poor laborer:

> And his syre a soutere y-suled in grees
> His teeþ wiþ toylinge of leþer tatered as a sawe!
> Alaas! þat lordes of þe londe leueþ swiche wrechen,
> And leneþ swiche lorels for her lowe workes![29]

A feudal conservative like Langland, the poet thus uses his plowman as an ideological figurehead to reassert the proper place and work of commons.

Peres also asserts, like Langland, that the measure of clerical holiness is work and its fruits. Peres notes that while the friars' orders were founded in truth, love and humility and were "Grounded on þe godspell,"[30] they now overturn the truth through their double-talk and glosing:

> But now þe glose is so greit in gladding tales
> Þat turneþ vp twp-folde vnteyned opon trewþe
> Þat þei bene cursed of Crist y can hem well proue;
> Wiþ-outen his blissinge bare beþ þey in her werkes.[31]

Just after the wanderer quotes Christ from Matthew 7:20, "by her fruyt men shall hem ful knowen,"[32] he comes upon the wealthy holdings of the Dominicans. The fruit of the Dominicans' work, their worldly wealth, serves as a sign of their spiritual poverty, just as the patient poverty of the plowman is a sign of his spiritual wealth.

Praising Wyclif for warning corrupt clerics, the poet thus enlists Piers in support of the Wycliffite cause just as the 1381 rebels added Piers to their own ranks as a signal of their moral authority.[33] But rather than anticipating a comprehensive social renovation, the poet of *Peres the Ploughmans Crede* only advocates Wycliffite reforms, the most prominent of which is the translation of key Christian texts into English so that the commons can learn about and better live their faith; in fact, the entire search of the wanderer to learn his creed culminates in a fairly accurate English translation of the Apostles' Creed. The poem thus asserts Wyclif's program for sacred texts in English so that Christians other than clerics could read the Bible, and a primary reason for this movement is the very glosing of scripture that Langland and the author of *Peres the Ploughmans Crede* condemn. If Christians could not trust clerics to interpret sacred texts, then individuals needed to read such texts themselves; the first move toward a more general readership for the Bible was, of course, its availability in the vernacular. We see the groundwork for such a readership in the semi-literate wanderers and plowmen of *Piers Plowman, Peres the Plowman's Crede* and *The Complaint of the Ploughman*, which features a wandering plowman whom a pelican asks to record the debate between the church and its critics. Like Langland's Will, the wanderer in search of the Creed is not completely illiterate, as he tells us:

> A and all myn A.b.c. after haue y lerned,
> And patred in my pater-noster iche poynt after oþer,
> And after all, myn Aue-marie almost to þe ende;
> But all my kare is to comen for y can nohȝt my Crede.[34]

Although his Latin is not even good enough for him to have learned the entire *Ave Marie*, the wanderer wishes for instruction on the tenets of his faith and on the way a Christian should live, but the representatives of the Church refuse to teach him either by word or deed. The poet never suggests that the friars do not actually know the creed themselves, only that they would rather quickly absolve sinners and collect money and goods than instruct the wanderer. Controlling the keys not only to sacraments such as penance but to the Bible itself, clerics retained the power to forgive, condemn, and interpret, and their abuse of such powers clearly motivates the satire and criticism of *Peres the Ploughmans Crede* and *The Complaint of the Ploughman.*[35]

But while the author of *Peres the Plowman's Crede* supports Wyclif's calls for reform and vernacular texts, he reaffirms the tenets of Christian belief in the Plowman's Creed, including the matter of transubstantiation, to suggest that neither he nor other Wycliffites are actually heretical, but only persecuted by those who do the work of Satan from inside the Church like Langland's Antichrist Friar.[36] The pelican of *The Complaint of the Ploughman*, representing the Lollard point of view in opposition to the griffin, who represents the institutional Church, makes a similar claim, reaffirming orthodox belief while bitterly complaining that wealthy clerics are more interesting in cooking and fleecing their flocks than in guiding them; instead of protecting their sheep, these clerics use swords to butcher them.[37] As in *Peres the Plowmans Crede*, the representative of the Wycliffite position reaffirms the presence of Christ in the eucharist:

> His flesh and blood through his misterie
> Is there, in the forme of brede.
> How it is there it needeth not strive,
> Whether it be subget or accident,
> But as christ was when he was on live,
> So is he there verament.[38]

Refusing to accept the label of heretic, the poet asserts that he does not meddle with the articles of the faith, but only condemns those who pervert them for personal profit.

Employing both a wandering plowman and a pelican representative of the Lollard point of view, the poet of *The Complaint of the Ploughman* emphasizes the rift between the Church and its critics, in contrast with Langland's vision of a more comprehensive and millenarian social regeneration. Once again, seeking the "high way" represents the attempt to follow the path of Christ, and refusing to follow that path designates one as part of the company of Antichrist:

> Loke how many among hem all
> Holden not this hie waie;
> With Antichrist they shullen fall,
> For they wullen god betraie.[39]

But instead of anticipating apocalyptic justice on a social scale, the poet emphasizes individual judgment after death for traitor clerics:

Alas! who may such saints call,
That wilneth welde earthly honour,
As low as Lucifere such shal fall
In balefull blackesse to builden her boure;
That eggeth the people to errour,
And maketh them to hem thrall;
To Christ I hold such a one traitour,
As low as Lucifer such one shall fall.[40]

As his predecessors did, this poet asserts that the people can tell whether the clerics are traitors or not by observing their works: For they ne ben but counterfete, / Man may know hem by her fruite."[41] As in *Peres the Plowmans Crede*, the sharp contrast of clerical ideals with corrupt practices points up the perversity of such false followers of Christ, who "laieth our her large nettes, / For to take silver and gold; / Fillen coffers, and sackes fettes, / There as they soules catch shold."[42] Instead of working as fishers of men as Jesus charged the apostles, instead of converting work for material profit into work for spiritual salvation, corrupt clerics use their vocations to collect earthly goods. The griffin gloses, trying to justify the Church's wealth as a sign of dignity and God's approbation and asserting, "Ech man shall live by his travaile, / Who best doeth shall have most mede."[43] The lollard pelican, however, rebuts the griffin and defends the true Church by reaffirming poverty and spiritual treasure over material wealth:

Her rich clothing shall be rightwisenesse;
Her treasure true life shall be;
Charity shall be her richesse;
Her lordship shall be unité;
Hope in God her honesté;
Her vessel cleane conscience;
Poore in spirit and humilité
Shall be holy churches defence.[44]

According the pelican, rather than being sons of God, greedy clerics are "hired men" who do the work of the devil for payment and who drive their sheep into the desert instead of helping them.[45] In doing so, the clergy does the work of Satan and can thus be called Antichrists, an epithet which the poet of *The Complaint of the Ploughman* uses effectively as an indicator of moral depravity in an *ad hominem* attack. The poet directly defines an Antichrist as anyone who perverts the word and work of Christ:

> What is Antichrist to say,
> But even Christs adversarie?
> Such hath now ben many a day,
> To Christs bidding ful contrarie,
> That from the truth cleane varry,
> Out of the way they ben wend,
> And Christs people untruly carry;
> God for his pitie amend.[46]

As the adversary of Christ and his poor—in this poem, the Lollard constituency represented by the pelican and persecuted by the Antichrist Church for trying to follow Christ—the griffin's unnatural and destructive power further identifies the corrupt institutional Church as the instrument of Satan. Half ravenous lion and half bird, which "betokeneth pride, / As Lucifer, that high flew was,"[47] the griffin calls on other birds of his company, representing various orders, to tear apart the pelican,[48] but the pelican returns with the phoenix, Christ, who avenges the pelican by slaying and casting down the griffin and his company.[49]

Although the vengeance of the phoenix represents Christ's final judgment of evil clerics, the poem is eschatological and chiliastic, but not millenarian in character, for the poem says nothing of a renovated society of honest, meek birds. When Christ the phoenix tears apart the birds of prey, their punishment is not necessarily earthly, but possibly reserved for the next world. Rather than issuing an urgent apocalyptic warning for the general population, the author of *The Complaint of the Ploughman* focuses on his clerical targets and emphasizes their punishment with the stated purpose of reforming their behavior.[50]

Mum and the Soothsegger is the final poem from around the turn of the century that is clearly derivative of *Piers Plowman*.[51] Rather than targeting the clergy as the underlying cause of fourteenth-century society's evils, the poet performs a *post mortem* on Richard II's reign and charges nobles and social climbers with devastating the kingdom. Again we see a wanderer searching for truth, in this case a "soothsegger" to decry oblivious and self-absorbed nobles, the retinues they maintain, and ostentatious social climbers, but wherever he goes, he finds instead the company of Mum, who will not speak the truth, whether out of fear or greed. More political satire than moral statement, the poem asserts that the truth-speaker can expect, like the pelican of *The Complaint of the Ploughman*, that those he criticizes always try to tear him apart, that they "al to-teereth his toppe for his trewe tales."[52]

Although the poet primarily criticizes political and legal targets, he does not neglect corrupt clerics entirely, for he adopts the Wycliffite commonplace that the four orders of friars are the kin of Cain, with each letter of the medieval spelling "CAIM" representing one of the orders: Carmelite, Augustinian, Iacobin (Dominican), and Minorite. Adapting Langland's metaphor of Jesus the knight jousting with the pharisees, and echoing the argument of the poor plowman of *Peres the Ploughmans Crede* that friars are like pharisees,[53] the poet of *Mum and the Soothsegger* asserts that the friars, instead of being "knights of conscience" have "ioygned in iustes agayns Ihesus werkes."[54] The poet never anticipates an imminent earthly battle between Jesus and his opponents, but diverts to a dream-vision to suggest the fate of those who oppose Christ and the common good. Those who work against the common good, the weeds and harmful insects in the garden and the drones of the hive, are destroyed by the man in white, a gardener and hive-keeper remarkably like the figure clothed in white of John's Apocalypse. Entering the garden, the dreamer starts to pull at fruit and then sees the man:

> An olde auncyen man of a hunthrid wintre,
> Y-weded in white cloþe and wisely y-made,
> With hore heres on his heede more þanne half white,
> A faire visaige and a vresse and vertuous to sene.
> His eyen were al ernest, eggid to noon ille,
> With a broode besmet berde / ballid a lite
> As comely a creature as euer kinde wrought.[55]

While the figure represents God the creator, for he asserts "þe grovnde is myn owen," he also does the work of Piers; he tends the garden "Forto digge and to delue and to do suche deedes / As longeth to þis leyȝttone."[56] A creature created by "kinde," Piers, the true Christian worker, is as close to God in deed as possible, a sign of God working through man and man working for God and his people, a conflation of Piers and the incarnate Christ similar to the one we find in Langland's poem. This gardener, like Piers who calls down Hunger to punish those who would not work, seeks to punish "wastours" who threaten the common good: "And wormes þat worchen not but wasten my herbes, / I daisshe þaym to deeth and delue oute þaire dennes."[57] Within the hive, the poet's model for perfectly ordered society, the queen is the King, those who serve him by gathering nectar and building chambers are true workers, and drones who haunt the hive only to fill their stomachs with honey are *wastours* to be destroyed. Although the poet avoids the suggestion of apocalyptic battle, the *locus amoenus* through which the dreamer roams, a landscape of perfect woods, hills, hedges, mansions, new-mown meadows, newly reaped fields of grain, and gardens is a millennial landscape, a vision of perfect agricultural life, a land flowing with honey from which all who threaten the common good are cast. Asserting the ideal of steady stewardship, the poet looks to a new world, a new century and a new royal household; when the wanderer awakens, he validates his dream:

> Hit ferde as a fairye / but feithfully þe wordes
> Were ful wise of þe wye in þe white cloþes,
> And eeke nedeful and notable for þis new world.
> And eeke plaisant to my pay / for þay putten me to rest
> Of my long labour and litryng aboute,
> For he provid by profitable poyntz and fele
> That the sothe-sigger shuld haue þe better
> Of Mvm, and þe maistrie, malgre his chekes.[58]

In the hope that Henry IV will learn from the mistakes of his predecessor, the poet employs millenarian imagery to proclaim the renovation of political, legal, and economic society. Like Langland and the 1381 rebels, the poet imagines that society's renewal must be accomplished through the person of the king, who will restore the traditional feudal structure and thus reorder society. But while he employs millenarian imagery, the poet of *Mum and the Soothsegger* rejects the interpetation of old prophecies and characterizes apocalyptic thinking as foolish and dangerous. While discussing the strife of the previous forty years, he notes that people become "halfe a-masid" by misconstruing prophecies. In a reference perhaps to John Ball and the 1381 uprising, the poet notes the futility of foreseeing the weather, let alone of correctly interpreting prophetic or apocalyptic signs:

> For þere mys wight in þis world þat wote bifore eue
> How þe wind and þe wedre wol wirche on þe morowe,

> Ne noon so cunnyng a clerc þat construe wel couthe
> Ere sunneday a seuenyght what shal falle,
> Thus þay muse on þe mase on mone and on sterres
> Til heedes been hewe of and hoppe on þe grene,
> And al þe wide world wondre on þaire workes.[59]

Recognizing the link between apocalyptic movements and violence, the poet of *Mum and the Soothsegger* urges practical and legal reform in the face of economic and social upheaval.

Although the poems of his imitators do not exhibit the apocalyptic urgency of Langland's work or the rebel communications of 1381, they rely on Langland's figure of the plowman as the symbol of the ideal Christian worker and as a foil for contemporary corruption. As indices of economic, political, and religious discontent, all of these poems respond to the challenges of their age within the apocalyptic framework of history, whether their working model is eschatological, regenerative, or some combination of the two. In each case, the vision of a reformed or ideal society is based on the only political and economic system with which the rebels and poets had experience: the feudal system. Projecting an ideal vision of a perfect past into the future and seeking to reform society, these rebels and poets, while not all conservative in action, showed signs of nostalgia that led them to reaffirm traditional feudal ideology. To the extent that Langland, the 1381 rebels, and Langland's imitators express nostalgia for a golden past on which they base their hopes of a reformed world, they practice an economy of culture, a reiteration of the values, social myths, and sense of justice of the past in the context of a world renewed.

NOTES

INTRODUCTION

1. John A. Yunck, *The Lineage of Lady Meed: The Development of Mediaeval Venality Satire* (Notre Dame: University of Notre Dame Press, 1963), 190.

2. Ibid., 258.

3. Lester K. Little, *Religious Poverty and the Profit Economy in Medieval Europe* (Ithaca: Cornell, University, Press, 1978), 41.

4. Yunck, 284.

5. *Piers Plowman*: The B Version, ed. by George Kane and E. T. Donaldson (London: University of London, Athlone Press, 1975), Prol. 16.

6. See Norman Cohn, *The Pursuit of the Millennium: Revolutionary Messianism in Medieval and Reformation Europe and Its Bearing on Modern Totalitarian Movements*, 2d ed., Harper Torchbooks, The Academy Library, ed. Benjamin Nelson (New York: Harper & Row, 1961), where the author points out the relationship between economic and demographic change and the incidence of chiliasm: "The areas in which the age-old prophecies about the Last Days took on a new revolutionary meaning and a new, explosive force were the areas of rapid social change—and not simply change but expansion: areas where trade and industry were developing and where the population was rapidly increasing. Life in such areas differed vastly from the agricultural life which was the norm throughout the thousand-year span of the Middle Ages" (22).

7. Ibid., 14–15.

8. Ibid., 30.

9. Ibid.

10. Ibid., 24.

11. Rodney Hilton, *Bondmen Made Free: Medieval Peasant Movements and the English Rising of 1381* (London: Routledge, 1973), 174.

12. Hilton, 174–175. Hilton points out the relationship between rebellious activity and the growing capitalist economy: "the leading social force in medieval peasant movements, even the most radical, seems to have been those elements most in contact with the market, those who in suitable circumstances would become capitalist farmers" (235).

13. Ibid., 174.

14. Ibid., 166.

15. Ibid., 233.

16. Ibid.

17. Cohn, *In Pursuit of the Millennium*, 32.

18. Harry A. Miskimin, *The Economy of Early Renaissance Europe 1300–1460* (Englewood Cliffs, N.J.: Prentice-Hall, Inc., 1969), 3.

19. Ibid.

20. Hilton, 212.

21. Harry Miskimin, "Monetary Movements and Market Structure: Forces for Contraction in Fourteenth- and Fifteenth-Century England," *Cash, Credit and Crisis in Europe, 1300–1600* (London: Variorum Reprints, 1989; reprint *The Journal of Economic History* XXIV, Baltimore, 1964), 470.

22. K. Polanyi and C. Arensberg, *Trade and Market in the Early Empires* (Glancoe, 1957), 74, quoted in Jacques Le Goff, *Your Money or Your Life: Economy and Religion in the Middle Ages*, trans. Patricia Ranum. (New York: Zone Books, 1988), 20.

23. Ibid.

24. Walter W. Skeat, Introduction to *The Vision of William Concerning Piers the Plowman, In Three Parallel Texts, Together with Richard the Redeless, By William Langland* (London: Oxford University Press, 1886; reprinted 1924), Vol II, lv.

CHAPTER ONE

1. Walter W. Skeat, Introduction to *The Vision of William Concerning Piers the Plowman,* Vol II, lvi.

2. Ibid.

3. Morton W. Bloomfield, *Piers Plowman as a Fourteenth-Century Apocalypse* (New Brunswick, NJ: Rutgers University Press, 1961), 107.

4. See Augustine's *Confessions*, X–XI.

5. Raymond Williams, *Keywords: A Vocabulary of Culture and Society*, (New York: Oxford University Press, 1983), 251.

6. Bloomfield, 104–5.

7. Kathryn Kerby-Fulton, *Reformist Apocalypticism and "Piers Plowman,"* Cambridge Studies in Medieval Literature 7 (Cambridge: Cambridge University Press, 1990).

8. C. A. Patrides, *The Phoenix and the Ladder: The Rise and Decline of the Christian View of History* (Berkeley: University of California Press, 1964), 9.

9. The movement of soul as Plato describes it in the *Timaeus* is cyclical: its circular movement repeats with each incarnation. The Christian neoplatonists most likely abbreviated this cyclical pattern to one closed circle so as not to suggest belief in reincarnation.

10. N. F. Blake, Introduction to *The Phoenix*. Manchester: Manchester University Press, 1964; reprint, Exeter: University of Exeter Press; Short Run Press, Ltd., 1990, 8–10 (page references are to reprint edition).

11. Ibid., 12–19.

12. Cohn, 3.

13. Patrides, 6.

14. Ibid.

15. Ibid.

16. Introduction to Ecclesiastes, *The Jerusalem Bible*, Reader's Edition (Garden City, NY: Doubleday & Company, 1966), 854.

17. See Eccl. 11:7–12:7.

18. Apoc. 20:4. Unless otherwise noted, all Biblical quotations follow the Douay-Rheims Version, revised by Bishop Richard Challoner, 1749–1752 (Baltimore: John Murphy Company, 1899; repr., Rockford, Illinois: TAN Books and Publishers, 1971).

19. The persecutor at the time the book of Daniel was written (c. 165 B.C.) was Antiochus Epiphanes, whose invasion of Israel sparked the Maccabean rebellion of 1 Maccabees. The portrait of Antiochus in Daniel (11:21–39; 8:23–26) was interpreted as a description of Antichrist by later readers. Daniel's vision of the "one of great age" and of the son of man provided a scriptural basis for John's description of Judgment Day in Revelation. Compare the heavenly court of judgment and the record books of Daniel 7:9–10 and Apoc. 20:11–12.

20. Daniel 7:13–14.

21. Cohn, 44–45.

22. In Matthew 22:23–33 the Sadducees, whom the gospel notes denied that there would be a resurrection, try to trick Jesus with questions about family relationships after the resurrection. Jesus replies that "in the resurrection they shall neither marry nor be married; but shall be as the angels of God in heaven." Cf., Luke 20:27–38.

23. In the Bread of Life discourse of John 6:35–58, for example, Jesus repeatedly promises eternal life for those who believe in the Son: "I will raise him up in the last day."

24. Matt. 25:31–42.

25. Matt. 25:35, 42–43.

26. Langland makes frequent use of biblical expressions, mainly "Judge not, that you may not be judged" (Matt. 7:1; cf., Luke 6:37) and "Vengeance is mine says the Lord" (see Deut. 32:35; Rom. 12:19; Heb.10:30.) to warn against judging and punishing others. See *Piers Plowman* B.VI.227; X.209; X.374; XI.90; XI.107; XII.89; and XIX.447 for Langland's use of these and similar expressions.

27. *Piers Plowman* B.Prol. 17.

28. Paul tells followers to prepare for a new dawn: "it is now the hour for us to rise from our sleep. For now our salvation is nearer than when we believed. The night is passed, and the day is at hand. Let us therefore cast off the works of darkness, and put on the armour of light" (Rom. 13:11–12). Hebrews 10:37 also urges the newly converted to persevere and prepare: "For yet a little and a very little while, and he that is to come, will come, and will not delay." John too seeks to prepare followers for the end of the world: "Little children, it is the last hour; and as you have heard that Antichrist cometh, even now there are become many Antichrists: whereby we know that it is the last hour" (1 John 2:18).

29. In his sermon on the end times in Matt. 24:15–31, Jesus tells his disciples the signs of the coming of the Son of Man: destruction, including the destruction of the Temple, war, earthquakes, famine, and persecution followed by the darkening of the sun and moon, the falling of the stars, the Son of Man coming in the clouds, and the gathering angels, who collect the chosen from the four winds, from one end of heaven to the other. Cf., Mark 13:24–27, Luke 21:25–28.

30. 2 Peter 3:10.

31. Matt. 24:34–36; cf. Mark 13:33–37. Luke 9:27 also supports the idea that the kingdom is at hand: "But I tell you of a truth: There are some standing here that shall not taste death, till they see the kingdom of God."

32. For example, in 2 Peter 3:3–18 the apostle responds to scorners who ask, "Where is his promise or his coming? for since the time that the fathers slept, all things continue as they were from the beginning of the creation," asserting that "the heavens and the earth which are now . . . are kept in store, reserved unto fire against the day of judgment and perdition of the ungodly men." Peter then offers another explanation for the delay: "But of this one thing be not ignorant, my beloved, that one day with the Lord is as a thousand years, and a thousand years as one day. The Lord delayeth not his promise, as some imagine, but dealeth patiently for your sake, not willing that any should perish, but that all should return to penance. But the day of the Lord shall come as a thief, in which the heavens shall pass away with great violence, and the elements shall be melted with heat, and the earth and the works which are

in it, shall be burnt up" (2 Peter 8–10). Peter concludes his second letter by urging Christians to live holy and saintly lives while they wait.

33. Cohn provides an excellent example of early Christian belief in the millennial garden with his translation of Apostolic Father Papias (born c. A.D. 60), *De expositione oraculorum dominicorum (fragments)* in *Patrilogiae cursus completus, series Graeca,* Vol V., cols. 1258–1259: "The days will come in which vines shall appear, having each ten thousand shoots, and on every shoot ten thousand twigs, and on each true twig ten thousand stems, and on every stem ten thousand bunches, and in every bunch ten thousand grapes, and every grape will give five-and-twenty metretes of wine. And when any one of the Saints shall take hold of a bunch, another bunch shall cry out, 'I am a better bunch, take me; bless the Lord through me.' Likewise (the Lord) said that a grain of wheat would bear ten thousand grains, and every grain give ten pounds of the finest flour, clear and pure; and apples and seeds and grass would produce in similar proportions; and all animals, feeding only on what they received from the earth, would become peaceable and friendly to each other, and completely subject to man" (10–11).

34. Cohn, 11.

35. Cohn, 11 translates Irenaeus, *Adversus haereses* lib. V, cap. xxxii–xxxiv, col. 1210 in *Patrilogiae cursus completus, series Graeca*: "For God is rich in all things, and all things are his. It is fitting, therefore, that the creation itself, being restored to its primeval condition, should without qualification be under the dominion of the righteous" (11).

36. Cohn, 12. Condensed from Lactantius Firmianus, *Divinae Institutiones*, lib. VII, cap. xx, xxiv, xxvi.

37. After predicting that only a remnant will survive the great destruction that Yahweh has decreed because of His peoples' arrogance, Isaiah describes the coming of a virtuous judge and king and the world over which he will reign: "The wolf shall dwell with the lamb: and the leopard shall lie down with the kid: the calf and the lion, and the sheep shall abide together, and a little child shall lead them. The calf and the bear shall feed: their young ones shall rest together: and the lion shall eat straw like the ox. And the suckling child shall play on the hole of the asp: and the weaned child shall thrust his hand into the den of the basilisk" (Isaiah 11:6–8).

38. Cohn, 13.

39. Chapter 6.20 of Augustine, *Commentary on the Lord's Sermon on the Mount with Seventeen Related Sermons*, trans. Denis J. Kavanagh, O.S.A. (New York: Fathers of the Church, Inc., 1951), 128.

40. R. E. Kaske, *Medieval Christian Literary Imagery: A Guide to Interpretation*, with Arthur Groos and Michael W. Twomey (Toronto: University of Toronto Press, 1988), 132–33. According to Kaske, the earliest commentaries, those of Nicholas Trevet, Thomas Walleys and John Ridevall, appeared in the first half of the fourteenth century and were copied into the sixteenth century.

41. Augustine, *The City of God* XVIII.54.

42. Ibid.

43. Peter Brown, *Augustine of Hippo: A Biography* (Berkeley and Los Angeles: University of California Press, 1967), 314.

44. Augustine, *Tractates on the Gospel of John* 19.5, The Fathers of the Church, trans. John W. Rettig, vol. 78 (Washington: The Catholic University of America Press, 1988), 153.

45. Augustine, *Tractates on the Gospel of John*, 22.13.2 quotes John 5:29, the basis of Piers's pardon: "And they who have done well shall come forth to the resurrection of life; they who have done ill, unto the resurrection of judgement" (210).

46. Augustine, *Tractates on the Gospel of John* 22.13, p. 209.

47. Ibid., 17.2, p. 109.

48. See Augustine's Sermon 109 on Matthew 5.25: "Only God knows when the end of the world will come. Now is the season of faith. I know not whether the end of the world will find any of us here. Perhaps it will not find us here. But the time is close at hand for every one of us, for we are mortal." Trans. Denis J. Kavanagh in *Commentary on the Lord's Sermon on the Mount with Seventeen Related Sermons,* (New York: The Fathers of the Church, 1951), 295.

49. Cohn, 14.

50. Such affinities are in part due to the influence of Greek philosophy on the Gospel of John.

51. When the introduction of Aristotle to the Latin West coincided with the rise of the universities in the second half of the twelfth century, study of his works largely eclipsed the neoplatonic movement in academic circles. Robert Grosseteste developed one of the earliest forms of university Aristotelianism, also known as Augustinian or Neoplatonic Aristotelianism, at Oxford. References to light and illumination pervade Augustinian Aristotelianism, reinforcing medieval dualism.

52. Winthrop Wetherbee, *Platonism and Poetry in the Twelfth Century: The Literary Influence of the School of Chartres* (Princeton: Princeton University Press, 1972), 30. Wetherbee also lists the treatises of Apuleius and anonymous works such as the Hermetic *Asclepius* as texts "valued largely for the insights they provided into the meaning of Plato's cosmology" (30).

53. Ibid.

54. Ibid., 42.

55. "Boece," *The Works of Geoffrey Chaucer*, ed. F.N. Robinson (Boston: Houghton Mifflin Company, 1957) III.m.2. 39–46.

56. Chauncer uses the cyclical patterns of nature and of pilgrimage in *The Canterbury Tales,* and the form of the roundel at the end of Chaucer's *Parlement of Foules* reinforces the circular pattern of Nature from year to year. Nature in Alain de Lille's *De planctu naturae*, a descendent of Boethius's Lady Philosophy, descends from the heavens with a sparkling crown of gems around her head that represents the cosmos. The gems produce harmonious music, emit light, and circle like the planets.

57. Kerby-Fulton, 12.

58. A. C. Spearing, *Medieval Dream-Vision Poetry* (Cambridge: Cambridge University Press, 1976), 4.

59. Other medieval works that exhibit some or all of these commonplaces include the work of Dante, the *Roman de la Rose*, *Wynnere and Wastour*, and *Pearl.* Parodying apocalyptic and visionary conventions, Chaucer probably demonstrates the greatest innovation in his use of apocalyptic commonplaces in his dream-visions when he employs a little dog in *The Book of the Duchess* and a huge eagle in *The House of Fame* as authoritative figures and guides.

60. Cohn, 99.

61. Marjorie Reeves, *Joachim of Fiore and the Prophetic Future* (London: SPCK, 1976), 57.

62. Ibid.

63. Ibid., 20.

64. Ibid., 19–20. The spiral or gyre becomes a conventional means of explaining the course of history. Yeats, for example, adopts this scheme, with each closing of an old and opening of a new spiral signifying the end and beginning of a new millennium.

65. Cohn, 100–101.

66. Cohn, 55 explains that some believers claimed that Charlemagne rose from the dead to help with the Crusades, while according to others, Charlemagne only slept in a vault awaiting his time to return.

67. *Pearl* in *The Poems of the Pearl Manuscript*, ed. Malcolm Andrew and Ronald Waldron (Berkeley and Los Angeles: University of California Press, 1978), lines 939–48.

68. Ibid., lines 66–84.

69. A. C. Spearing in *Medieval Dream-Poetry* describes the typical dream-vision landscape, in which we can see both the Christian and pagan traditions at work. The *locus amoenus* "became the heavenly landscape of literary visions and dream . . . . set in bright southern sunlight (perhaps augmented by or transformed into the jewelled brilliance of the Apocalypse), but it also provides shade against the sum, and is therefore furnished with a tree or trees, often fruit-trees. The trees will be in a flowery meadow, which will provide fragrance as well as bright colours, and there will probably be birds singing in them, (though

in some cases the place of birds is taken by human or angelic song). In the meadow there is almost invariably a spring or brook, often rising from a fountain, and there will usually be a breeze" (17–18).

70. *Pearl*, lines 37–47.

71. Ibid., lines 29–35.

72. One important source for such imagery is the Book of Revelation: "And another angel came out from the temple crying with a loud voice to him that sat upon the cloud: thrust in thy sickle, and reap, because the hour is come to reap: for the harvest of the earth is ripe. And he that sat on the cloud thrust his sickle into the earth, and the earth was reaped. And another angel came out from the altar, who had power over fire; and he cried with a loud voice to him that had the sharp sickle, saying: Thrust in thy sharp sickle, and gather the clusters of the vineyard of the earth; because the grapes thereof are ripe. And the angel thrust in his sharp sickle into the earth, and gathered the vineyard or the earth, and cast it into the great press of the wrath of God: And the press was trodden without the city, and blood came out of the press, up to the horses' bridles, for a thousand and six hundred furlongs" (Apoc. 14:15–20). Also in this tradition is Matthew 13:24–30, in which both good seeds and cockles of the Kingdom of God are allowed to grow together until harvest, when the cockles are bound and burned and the wheat is reaped gathered into the barn, a clear analogy to the separation of the sheep and goats at the Final Judgment. For a brief history of Judeo-Christian agricultural imagery, see Bloomfield, 106–7.

Chapter Two

1. James Simpson, "Spirituality and Economics in Passus 1–7 of the B Text," *Yearbook of Langland Studies 1* (1987): 85.

2. The expression "Pay what you owe" has several biblical sources. Jesus advises, "Render therefore to Caesar the things that are Caesar's; and to God the things that are God's" (Matt. 22:21; cf., Mark 12:17, Luke 20:25). Ecclesiastes 5:3 asserts, "If thou hast vowed any thing to God, defer not to pay it: for an unfaithful and foolish promise displeaseth him: but whatsoever thou hast vowed, pay it." In Matthew 18:23–35, the phrase indicates not the inexorable nature of justice expressed in Exodus 21:24, "Eye for eye, tooth for tooth, hand for hand, foot for foot," but instead stresses the generosity and forgiveness of God, Jesus' expectations for his followers, and God's punishment for those he forgives who then exact payment from their own debtors. According to the parable, after a lord forgave his servant a debt of ten thousand talents, the servant throttled a fellow servant who owed him a hundred pence, saying, "Pay what you owe" (Matt. 18:28). When the lord learned that the servant cast his fellow debtor into prison, he called him back, blamed the servant for failing to show the same compassion he had been shown, and "delivered him to the torturers until he paid all the debt" (Matt. 18:34). While the expression "pay what you owe" is thus a principle of justice, in the parable it also indicates that Christ has already paid the debt of Christians, that their debts, no matter how big, are forgiven if they faithfully follow Christ's example.

3. Bloomfield, 130. Also see Robert Worth Frank, Jr. *"Piers Plowman" and the Scheme of Salvation: An Interpretation of Dowel, Dobet, and Dobest,* Yale Studies in English 136 (New Haven: Yale University Press, 1957), 100–107.

4. Ibid.

5. Jacques Le Goff, *Your Money or Your Life: Economy and Religion in the Middle Ages*, trans. Patricia Ranum (New York: Zone Books, 1988), 42. Le Goff, 69–70 challenges traditional economic histories and analyses of the medieval economy, claiming that such reconstructions are "especially ineffective for the Middle Ages, because at that time the Church had no economic doctrine, and there were no economic thinkers." Instead of analyzing economic data, Le Goff's study on the moral and legal status of usurers explores how the teachings of the Church slowed the development of capitalism.

6. *Piers Plowman* B.XIX.191–98.

7. Lawrence M. Clopper, "Need Men and Women Labor?" in *Chaucer's England: Literature in Historical Context*, ed. Barbara Hanawalt, Medieval Studies at Minnesota, vol. 4 (Minneapolis: University of Minnesota Press, 1992), 115.

8. *Piers Plowman* B.Prol.112–22.

9. See G. R. Owst, "The 'Angel' and the 'Goliardeys' of Langland's Prologue," *Modern Language Review* 20:3 (July 1925): 270–79. Owst notes that Langland's "political ideal is the commonwealth as it exists, only with each part working as it was meant to do."

10. *Piers Plowman* B.Prol.146.

11. Ibid., Prol.17–32.

12. Ibid., X.397–98.

13. Ibid., Prol.92–96.

14. See Acts 8:9–24. Peter clearly rebukes Simon for his offer of money in return for the power to lay hands on people so that they receive the Holy Spirit: "Keep thy money to thyself, to perish with thee, because thou hast thought that the gift of God may be purchased with money. Thou hast no part nor lot in this matter. For thy heart is not right in the sight of God" (Acts 8:20-21).

15. *Piers Plowman* B.Prol.67.

16. Ibid., X.311–21.

17. Ibid., Prol.61.

18. Ibid., Prol.62–67.

19. Ibid., XX.332.

20. Ibid., XX.364–67.

21. Ibid., XX.372.

22. Ibid., XX.368.

23. Lester K. Little, *Religious Poverty and the Profit Economy in Medieval Europe* (Ithaca: Cornell University Press, 1978), 200–201. Little continues: "There is an early Franciscan allegorical work on poverty entitled the *Holy Commerce* (*Sacrum Commercium*), or, as a fourteenth-century writer once called it, *The Business of Poverty (Commercium Paupertatis)*."

24. Ibid., 201. Little summarizes J. H. Crehan, "Indulgences," *A Catholic Dictionary of Theology*, III (London, 1971) 84–90.

25. Little, 181. The scholastic consideration of contemporary social and economic problems reflects a change in attitudes towards economic and institutional life that according to Little signal an evolution "from the grudging approval by the Church Fathers of the state as a necessary evil, to the full scholastic acceptance" of private property and of the state's natural and good character (177). Le Goff reports that the schoolmen even worked to legitimize the work of merchants and some moneylenders by determining that there were five "excuses" for making a profit: 1) penalty for late payment, 2) the possibility of greater legitimate profit from investment elsewhere, 3) salary, 4) economic risk of losing the capital that one has lent, and 5) uncertainty in planning and calculations (73–74).

26. Little, 181.

27. Ibid., 188. Little credits Abelard's *Ethics*, subtitled *Know Thyself*, with providing the greatest challenge to the handbook system by increasing emphasis on intention. Little cites Alain de Lille's twelfth century *Liber poenitentialis,* in which the tarriffs of earlier penitentials disappeared and "the determination of appropriate penances was left entirely to the discretion of confessors," as evidence of the transition from one system of assigning penance to another (189). Little also discusses the role the friars played in the development of the sacrament: "The friars came forward with a new approach to confession and penance; they willingly entered into negotiation with the confessee to determine, through a series of questions and responses, the relative seriousness of the fault and hence the appropriate harshness of the penance" (199).

28. Le Goff, 11. The view that penitentials focused primarily on acts and not sinners is diputed by Allen J. Frantzen in *The Literature of Penance in Anglo-Saxon England*, (New Brunswick, NJ: Rutgers University Press, 1983), 7–11. Frantzen notes that the penitentials were only a guide for penalties and that confesssors often considered not only facts, but motives in determining penance (7). Nonetheless, the penitentials set normal penalties, or tariffs, for sins, and the move away from such manuals in the later Middle Ages removed these norms and thus increased the confessor's role in determining the appropriate penance for sinners.

29. Ibid.

30. Little, 179.

31. Ibid.

32. Le Goff, 42.

33. *Piers Plowman* B.X.357–67.

34. James 5:1–9.

35. The critical debate over this episode and what it suggests about the importance or irrelevance of works for salvation is too extensive to recount here. See Nevill K. Coghill "The Pardon of Piers Plowman," *Proceedings of the British Academy* 30 (1946): 303–57, reprinted in *Style and Symbolism in Piers Plowman: A Modern Critical Anthology,* Robert L. Blanch, ed. (Knoxville: University of Tennessee Press, 1969): 40–86; John Lawlor, "*Piers Plowman*: The Pardon Reconsidered" *Modern Language Review* 45:4 (October 1950): 449–58; Robert Worth Frank, Jr. "The Pardon Scene in *Piers Plowman*": *Speculum* 26:2 (April 1951) 317–31; Rosemary Woolf "The Tearing of the Pardon" in *Piers Plowman: Critical Approaches,* S. S. Hussey ed. (London: Methuen, 1969): 50–75, reprinted in Woolf *Art and Doctrine: Essays on Medieval Literature* (London: The Hambledon Press, 1986): 131–56; Mary C. Schroeder, "*Piers Plowman*: The Tearing of the Pardon," *Philological Quarterly* 49:1 (January 1970): 8–18; Susan H. McLeod "The Tearing of the Pardon in *Piers Plowman*" *Philological Quarterly* 56:1 (Winter 1977): 14–26; Denise N. Baker "From Plowing to Penitence: *Piers Plowman* and Fourteenth-Century Theology," *Speculum* 55:4 (October 1980): 715–25.

36. *Piers Plowman* B.XI.140–82. For the debate on the salvation of righteous heathens without benefit of baptism, see R. W. Chambers "Long Will, Dante, and the Righteous Heathen," *Essays & Studies* 9 (1924): 50–69; T. P. Dunning, "Langland and the Salvation of the Heathen" *Medium Ævum* 12 (1943): 45–54; Pamela Gradon, "*Trajanus Redivivus*: Another Look at Trajan in *Piers Plowman*," *Middle English Studies Presented to Norman Davis in Honour of His Seventieth Birthday*, Eds. Douglas Gray and E. G. Stanley (Oxford: Clarendon Press, 1983): 93–114; Gordon Whatley "The Uses of Hagiography: the Legend of Pope Gregory and the Emperor Trajan in the Middle Ages" *Viator* 15 (1984): 25–63.

37. Ibid., VI.232–37.

38. Ibid., XIX.201–49.

39. Ibid., XIX.250–55.

40. Rather than viewing *dowel*, *dobet*, and *dobest* as representative of the active, contemplative and mixed lives, I lean towards the position that the three are not separate ways of life, but cumulative. For the first position, see Henry W. Wells, "The Construction of *Piers Plowman*," *PMLA* 44:1 (March 1929): 123–49. For the argument that the trio are cumulative, see Nevill K. Coghill, "The Character of Piers Plowman Considered from the B Text," *Medium Ævum* 2:2 (June 1933): 54–86. Also see John F. Adams "Piers Plowman and the Three Ages of Man," *Journal of English and Germanic Philology* 61:1 (January 1962): 23–41, who argues that the trio correspond to phases in the dreamer's aging.

41. *Piers Plowman* B.XIX.108–23.

42. Ibid., XIX.124–81.

43. Ibid., XIX.182–87.

44. For a discussion of the role of social action in achieving Christian perfection, in progressing from *dowel* to *dobet* to *dobest*, see Chapter 5, which discusses how the English rebels used Langland's terminology as codewords for levels of preparation and action in the revolt.

45. Plowmen are described as working for the common good in England at least as early as Ælfric's *Colloquy on the Occupations*, in which the manager notes that everyone else has food and drink because of the plowman.

46. *Piers Plowman* B.VI.68.

47. Ibid. VI.74–77.

48. The pardon reads: "*Et qui bona egerunt ibunt in vitam eternam; / Qui vero mala in ignem eternum*" (VII.113–14).

49. Mary C. Schroeder (Carruthers) "*Piers Plowman*: The Tearing of the Pardon," *Philological Quarterly* 49:1 (January 1970) 8–18. Cf. Katherine Bache Trower "Temporal Tensions in the Vision of *Piers Plowman*," *Mediaeval Studies* 35 (1973) 389–412; Ruth M. Ames "The Pardon Impugned by the Priest," in *The Alliterative Tradition in the Fourteenth Century*, Bernard S. Levy and, Paul E. Szarmach, eds. (Kent State: Kent State University Press, 1981) 47–68.

50. *Piers Plowman* B.VII.124–25.

51. Ibid., VII.126–35.

52. Ibid., VII.115–18.

53. Ibid., VII.100–106.

54. Matt. 20:13–16.

55. Hebrews 9:11–14.

56. 1 Peter 1:18–20; cf. Isaiah 52:3, "For thus saith the Lord: You were sold gratis, and you shall be redeemed without money."

57. That money is "dead" is an important basis for the medieval condemnation of usury. Usury is an unnatural act, for money is not created to multiply naturally, as living creatures are. See note 62 below.

58. Little describes attitudes toward these occupational categories and discusses the growth of tertiary occupations in the later Middle Ages: "The bakers obviously produced something by their labour, and no one questioned that butchers, servants and water-carriers did hard work. They and the artisans and the industrial workers constituted the secondary sector of the society. The utterly new sector, however, consisted of those engaged in tertiary

occupations: the merchants, the bankers, the industrial entrepreneurs, and the professionals. This sector was dominant in urban life, not because it constituted a majority of the population in any one city, but because it was in the command of the new market economy and eventually derived therefrom considerable wealth and commensurate political power. The people in this sector did not appear to 'produce' anything. Ancestors of the modern 'white-collar workers', they manipulated words, or in some instances they sought to manipulate people through the use of words. They argued, they kept records, they drew up contracts, they negotiated, they bought and sold, they hired and fired, they told stories and sang, they lectured, and they wrote books and letters. They also listened and read, watched and were entertained" (24).

59. *Piers Plowman* B.IX.102–108. Sloth can recite rhymes of Robin Hood but does not know his Paternoster (V.394–95). Langland also warns knights and clergy from welcoming the king's minstrels and then turning away beggars, who are "goddes minstrales" (XIII.434–39).

60. Le Goff, 36–7.

61. Little explains the disreputable status of tertiary occupations: "Tradition was less unreservedly hostile to [urban activities other than usury] but still it cast doubt on their legitimacy. It did not, for example, regard the practice of law as dishonourable, but once lawyers started to collect fees some people wondered if lawyers had the right to sell advice and information. An analogous dilemma faces the masters who taught in the city schools; had they the right to sell knowledge, it was asked, since tradition taught that knowledge is a gift of God, whence it may not by sold" (39)?

62. According to Aquinas, money was only meant to be a medium of exchange. Le Goff cites the *Summa theologica* to illustrate the tradition behind the infertility of money: "Money is infertile, yet the usurer wants it to produce offspring. Having read Aristotle, Thomas Aquinas observes: 'Nummus non parit nummos' (Money does not reproduce itself) . . . . [I]t is against nature for money loaned to give birth to more money . . . . In the same vein, St. Bonaventure holds that money is intrinsically unproductive. 'In itself and by itself, money does not bear fruit but the fruit comes for elsewhere'" (29).

63. Little notes that teachers and lawyers legitimized their work by insisting they sold "their effort and their advice and their time, but not knowledge, which they consistently recognized was not theirs to sell" (177).

64. Le Goff, 28.

65. *Piers Plowman* B.X.476–82.

66. See Matt. 6:19–21, 19:21; Mark 10:21; Luke 12:33–34, 18:22. In Sermon 60.3 *On Almsgiving*, Augustine warns those who would fill their coffers that they do not know for whom they store up treasure, for they could die at any time.

67. *Piers Plowman* B.I.85.

68. Ibid., I.59.

98. For a discussion of the ironic use of *ynogh* to suggest excess see Jill Mann, "Satisfaction and Payment in Middle English Literature" *Studies in the Age of Chaucer* 5 (1983): 17–47.

99. *Piers Plowman* B.XX.51–55.

100. Adams, 283. Adams cites Gregory the Great's *Moralia in Iob* as the "ultimate source" of the Need passage and examines the doubleness of Need, true patient poverty and false worldliness, in Gregory's commentary on Leviathan. Adams also lists Proverbs 6:9–12 and Proverbs 30:8–9 as sources for understanding Need's place in the drama of the final days (287).

101. Ibid., 293.

102. Ibid., 294.

103. Ibid.

104. Kerby-Fulton, 5.

105. For the outrider monks of Passus X, for example, Clergy predicts harsh penance in an apocalyptic passage anticipating the coming of the just king and the advent of millenarian society:

Ac þer shal come a kyng and confesse you Religiouses,
And bete yow, as þe bible telleþ, for brekynge of youre rule,
And amend Monyals, Monkes, and Chanons,
And puten hem to hir penaunce, *Ad pristinum statum ire*;
And Barons wiþ Erles beten hem þoruȝ *Beatus vir*res techyng.
(*Piers Plowman* B.X.322–26)

CHAPTER THREE

1. Yunck, 190.

2. Ibid., 258.

3. Harry A. Miskimin, "Monetary Movements and Market Structure: Forces for Contraction in Fourteenth- and Fifteenth-Century England," *The Journal of Economic History* 24 (1964): 472. Reprinted in Miskimin, Harry A. *Cash, Credit and Crisis in Europe, 1300–1600*. Variorum Reprints: London, 1989. Miskimin begins this essay by describing two groups of historians, one which looks at declining trade figures, population, and production as evidence of a post-plague depression or recession, the other which looks to limited evidence such as increases in cloth exports as a sign of prosperity in the same period (470). Clearly, the sort of evidence one examines in large part determines the impression one gets about prosperity and poverty in this period. For this reason, Miskimin prefers to consider a wide range of economic data in his work, which affords us a wider perspective on the economic challenges of this period and promises a more balanced picture than studies that consider more limited economic data.

4. The difficult task of interpreting the array of data from this period is one reason that the work of Miskimin figures prominently throughout this chapter. While many economic historians remain proponents of their various theories, Miskimin makes a better case than most by synthesizing the complex and sometimes conflicting interpretations of the raw data.

5. Miskimin, "Monetary Movements and Market Structure," 482–83.

6. Ibid., 483.

7. Harry Miskimin, R.S Lopez, and A. Udovitch, "England to Egypt, 1350–1500: Long-term Trends and Long-distance Trade" *Cash, Credit and Crisis in Europe, 1300–1600* (London: Variorum Reprints, 1989; reprint *Studies in the Economic History of the Middle East*, ed. M.A. Cook, Oxford: Oxford UP, 1970), 94.

8. J. C. Russell, *British Medieval Population* (Albuquerque: University of New Mexico Press, 1948), 280.

9. *Piers Plowman* B.VI.183–90.

10. Helen Robbins, "A Comparison of the Effects of the Black Death on the Economic Organization of France and England," *Journal of Political Economy*, 36 (1928), 447–79; Harry A. Miskimin, *The Economy of Early Renaissance Europe 1300–1460* (Englewood Cliffs, N.J.: Prentice-Hall, Inc., 1969), 25–26; Harry A. Miskimin, R. S. Lopez, and A. Udovitch, "England to Egypt, 1350–1500," 96. Jean Gimpel also designates 1315–17 as the period of greatest famine in *The Medieval Machine: The Industrial Revolution of the Middle Ages*, 2d ed., (Cambridge: Cambridge University Press, Wildwood House Limited, 1988), 213.

11. Ibid., XIII.265–70.

12. Harry A. Miskimin, *The Economy of Early Renaissance Europe*, 80.

13. Ibid., 27.

14. Ibid., 97.

15. In *The Economy of Early Renaissance Europe,* Miskimin provides the following price index: "[I]f we take average prices during the period 1261–1350 as a base of 100, price levels for the next 50-year period, 1351–1400, are as follows. For metals, including lead, tin, solder, pewter, and brass, the index rises to 176; for textiles—here canvas, linen, and two types of woolen cloth—the index is 160; and finally, for agricultural implements, clouts, cloutnails, two types of wheels, ligatures, greatnails, hurdles, horseshoes, horseshoe nails, ploughshoes, and ploughshares, the index mounts to the enormous level of 235. These figures may be compared to aprice index of 99 for barley, peas, wheat, and rye, calculated on the same basis, for the second half of the fourteenth century. In the same period, the wages of building craftsmen increased by nearly 50 per cent" (89).

16. See Isaiah 2:4.

17. *Piers Plowman* B.III.305–10.

18. Thomas Walsingham, *Chronicon Angliae*. Ed. Edward Maunde Thompson. Rolls Series 64. London, 1874 depicts the rebels force as wielding shepherds' crooks and axes in addition to old, rusty swords, sooty (because long unused by the hearth) bows and arrows with sometimes only one feather: "*Quorum quidam tantum baculos, quidam rubigine obductos gladios, quidam bipennes solummodo, nonnulli arcus prae vetustate factos a fumo rubicundiores ebore antiquo, cum singulis sagittis, quarum plures contentae erant una pluma, ad regnum conquirendum convenere. Inter mille vero de talibus, de facili non videndus erat unus armatus, sed omnes, ut magnum numerum confecere, credevant totum regnum illis resistere non valere*" (286).

19. John Gower, *Confessio Amantis* V.11–21 in *The English Works of John Gower,* ed. G. C. Macaulay, vol. 1 (London: Oxford University Press, 1900), 402.

20. Miskimin, *The Economy of Early Renaissance Europe*, 90.

21. Ibid.

22. Hilton, 148.

23. Ibid., 149–50.

24. Harry Miskimin, "Money and Money Movements in France and England at the End of the Middle Ages" *Cash, Credit and Crisis in Europe, 1300–1600* (London: Variorum Reprints, 1989; reprint *Precious Metals in the Later Medieval and Early Modern Worlds*, ed. J. F. Richards, Durham: Carolina Academic Press, 1983), 80.

25. Ibid., 87.

26. Miskimin, *The Economy of Early Renaissance Europe*, 88. Miskimin explains that the Church benefitted in three ways from the plague: from a greater number of legacies; from larger individual bequests from those with no heirs, and from increased gifts from the living preparing for heaven.

27. Miskimin, "Monetary Movements and Market Structure," 483.

28. Ibid.

29. Miskimin, *The Economy of Early Renaissance Europe*, 41.

30. Ibid., 36–38.

31. Chaucer, General Prologue to *The Canterbury Tales*, 365–68.

32. Ibid., 453–73.

33. Miskimin relies on growing numbers of silken goods such as purses, girdles, hoods and belts from probate records to show the growing popularity of silk among the growing English upper middle class in *The Economy of Early Renaissance Europe*, 103.

34. *The Parson's Tale*, 415–19.

35. Ibid., 419.

36. Ibid., 420.

37. Ibid., 443–44.

38. Ibid., 443.

39. F. E. Baldwin, *Sumptuary Legislation and Personal Regulation in England* (Baltimore: The Johns Hopkins Press, 1926), 46–47. Quoted in Harry Miskimin, "Monetary Movements and Market Structure: Forces for Contraction in Fourteenth- and Fifteenth-Century England," 487.

40. Miskimin, "Monetary Movements and Market Structure," 487.

41. Ibid.

42. Miskimin, *The Economy of Early Renaissance Europe*, 122.

43. Ibid., 123.

44. Ibid., 125–28.

45. M. M. Postan, *Essays on Medieval Agriculture and General Problems of the Medieval Economy* (Cambridge: Cambridge University Press, 1973), 198.

46. Miskimin, *The Economy of Early Renaissance Europe*, 103.

47. Ibid., 122.

48. Ibid., 137.

49. *Piers Plowman* B.VI.9–14.

50. Ibid., VI.15–16.

51. N. J. Mayhew, "Numismatic Evidence and Falling Prices in the Fourteenth Century," *The Economic History Review* 2d ser., 27:1, 1974: 2.

52. Ibid.

53. Miskimin, *The Economy of Early Renaissance Europe*, 113. Miskimin agrees with Mayhew that the "technological limits of mineral exploitation were reached by the middle of the fourteenth century" (114).

54. Mayhew, 12, citing R. Ruding, *Annals of the Coinage of Great Britain and its Dependencies*, (1840), I, 200–15.

55. Harry Miskimin, "Monetary Movements and Market Structure," 473, citing R. Ruding *Annals of the Coinage of Britain and Its Dependencies*, 2d ed., II (London, 1819), 139.

56. Ibid., 473, citing Ruding 155.

57. Ibid., 473, citing Ruding 173.

58. Ibid., 473, citing Ruding 185–225.

59. Ibid., 474–75. Miskimin reports that in 1378–1379 Parliament "requested import prohibitions against cloth of gold, silk, handkerchiefs, precious stones, jewels, or furs and export prohibitions on wool unless the merchant, in each case, imported 10 per cent of its value in bullion."

60. Ibid., 478.

61. Mayhew, 3–4.

62. Miskimin, "Monetary Movements and Market Structure," 474.

63. Miskimin, *The Economy of Early Renaissance Europe*, 145.

64. Miskimin, "Monetary Movements and Market Structure," 477.

65. Harry Miskimin, "The Enforcement of Gresham's Law," *Cash, Credit and Crisis in Europe, 1300–1600* (London: Variorum Reprints, 1989; reprint "*Credito, banche e investimenti, secoli XIII–XX: Atti della quarta Settimana di studio*," *Prato,* 14–21 April 1972, *Instituo Internazionale di Storia Economica 'F.Datini.* Florence: Felice le Monnier, 1985), 155.

66. Ibid., 156.

67. Ibid., 153.

68. Mayhew, 13.

69. Michael Prestwich, "Early Fourteenth-Century Exchange Rates," *The Economic History Review* 2d ser., 32:4 (November 1979): 480.

70. Ibid., 477.

71. Ibid.

72. Miskimin, "The Enforcement of Gresham's Law," 149.

73. Miskimin, "Money and Money Movements in France and England at the End of the Middle Ages," 84.

74. Hilton, 153.

75. Hilton, 154.

76. Miskimin, *The Economy of Early Renaissance Europe*, 32.

77. Ibid., 33; 45.

78. Hilton, 152.

79. Miskimin, *The Economy of Early Renaissance Europe*, 33; 45.

80. Hilton, 152.

81. Miskimin, *The Economy of Early Renaissance Europe*, 50.

82. Hilton, 152.

83. Ibid.

84. Ibid., 152–53.

85. W. M. Ormrod, "The Peasants' Revolt and the Government of England," *Journal of British Studies* 29:1 (January 1990): 2–3.

86. Pamela Nightingale, "Capitalists, Crafts and Constitutional Change in Late Fourteenth-Century London," *Past & Present* 124 (August 1989): 11.

CHAPTER FOUR

1. *Middle English Dictionary,* ed. Hans Kurath. (Ann Arbor: University of Michigan Press, 1956). The first two entries for "compaignie" as "a professional group, such as a trade guild or an ecclesiastical body" (451) date from 1389 and appear in the *Norfolk Guild Returns*; the next use of the term in this sense appears in *The Canterbury Tales* in "The Man of Law's Tale," where Chaucer describes "a compaignye / Of chapmen riche" (B.134–35). Similarly, the *MED* entry for "felaushipe" indicates that the term was first used to designate a guild or craft fraternity in the Parliamentary Rolls of 1450 (462), and the entry for "felaue" shows it was used to mean "an associate in office, dignity, or work; a colleague, co-worker, partner" as early as c. 1300, but that its use increased with the growth of the guilds (460).

2. Williams, 291–95.

3. Chaucer, General Prologue to *The Canterbury Tales*, 363–64.

4. Sir Israel Gollancz, "Preface" in *A Good Short Debate Between Winner and Waster,* (Oxford University Press, 1921; repr., Cambridge, England: D.S. Brewer Ltd, 1974), C.1r.

5. Sir Israel Gollancz, ed. *A Good Short Debate Between Winner and Waster,* lines 1–7.

6. Ibid., lines 11–19.

7. Ibid., lines 290–93.

8. Ibid., line 256.

9. *Piers Plowman* B.III.285–322.

10. 2 Cor. 6:14–17.

11. See 1 John 1:3–10.

12. *Middle English Dictionary* and John A. Alford, *Piers Plowman: A Glossary of Legal Diction* (Cambridge: Brewer, 1988), 57. According to Alford, a *felawe* could be an accomplice, associate, or accessory to a crime. In "Chaucer and the Absent City" *Chaucer's England: Literature in Historical Context*, ed. Barbara Hanawalt, Medieval Studies at Minnesota, vol. 4 (Minneapolis: University of Minnesota Press, 1992), David Wallace makes a similar point concerning Chaucer's use of the term *meynee*, a "neutral term . . . that

is rarely implored in neutral contexts" (72) much like *felawe*: "specific *meynees* are generally figured as a force for good or evil, as constructive or destructive of social and moral order" (72–73).

13. Chaucer, *The Friar's Tale*, 1385.

14. *Piers Plowman* B.I.114.

15. Ibid., I.113.

16. Luke 10:1.

17. *Piers Plowman* B.XX.349.

18. Chaucer, *The Summoner's Tale*, 1740–1760.

19. In Luke, Jesus sends out his disciples: "And he said to them: The harvest is indeed great, but the labourers are few. Pray ye therefore the Lord of the harvest, that he send labourers into his harvest. Go: Behold I send you as lambs among wolves. Carry neither purse, nor scrip, nor shoes; and salute no man by the way" (Luke 10:2–4).

20. *Piers Plowman* B.XIX.258–99.

21. Ibid., II.210.

22. Ibid., V.99.

23. Ibid., VIII.23.

24. "Boece," *The Works of Geoffrey Chaucer*, ed. F. N. Robinson (Boston: Houghton Mifflin Company, 1957) IV.p.6.125–35.

25. Ibid., II.p.6.79–91.

26. Ibid., IV.p.3.78–79.

27. Ibid., IV.p.3.93–104.

28. Daniel 5 describes the transformation and its cause: "But when his heart was lifted up, and his spirit hardened unto pride, he was put down from the throne of his kingdom, and his glory was taken away. And he was driven out from the sons of men, and his heart was made like the beasts, and his dwelling was with the wild asses, and he did eat grass like an ox, and his body was wet with the dew of heaven: till he know that the most High rules in the kingdon of men, and that he will set over it whomsoever it shall please him" (20–21).

29. "Cleanness," *The Poems of the Pearl Manuscript,* ed. Malcolm Andrew and Ronald Waldron, York Medieval Texts, ser. 2 (Berkeley and Los Angeles: University of California Press), 1978, 1671–76.

30. Augustine, *On the Trinity (De trinitate)* 12.11 also describes how the moral degeneration of humans, especially the sin of pride, makes humans like beasts, dishonoring the image and likeness of God in human nature.

31. "Cleanness," 1681–86.

32. Ibid., 1688–1700:

By þat mony þik fytherez þryȝt ymbe his lyre,
Þat alle watz dubbed and dyȝt in þe dew of heuen;
Faxe, fyltered and felt, floȝed hym vmbe,
Þat schad fro his schulderes to his schere-wykes,
And twenty-folde twynande hit to his tos raȝt,
Þer mony clyuy as clyde hit clyȝt togeder.
His berde ibrad alle his brest to þe bare vrþe,
His browes bresed as breres aboute his brode chekes;
Holȝe were his yȝen and vnder campe hores,
And al watz gray as þe glede, with ful grymme clawres
Þat were croked and kene as þe kyte paune;
Erne-hwed he wtz and al ouerbrawden,
Til he wyst ful wel who wroȝt alle amyȝtes,
And cowþe vche kyndam tokerue and keuer when Hym lyked.

33. "Ywayn and Gawayn," *Five Middle English Narratives* ed. Robert D. Stevick (Indianapolis and New York: Bobbs-Merrill Company, 1967), 248; 561; 269. This speaking beast, more animal than man, has man's faculty of speech, but he is more brutal than the animals of the forest. The giant explains to Ywayn that he has the animals at his command, that he is "maister of hem alle" because he tortured animals with his strong fingers to make them wail and thus to frighten all the other animals into submission (295–312). When Ywayn goes mad from excessive, unreasonable mourning for his lady, he runs naked and wild through the woods, but he retains enough of his noble training to use a stolen bow and arrow to kill for food. Half man and half wild animal, Ywayn drinks the warm blood and eats the raw flesh of his prey until he stumbles on a hermit who will feed him like a stray dog at the door, giving him bread and water, cooking the animals Ywayn brought, and selling the skins to obtain better victuals for them both (1650–1708). Ywayn does not recover until a lady and her ladies-in-waiting recognize the noble knight sleeping naked under a tree and decide they must "him wynne into his wyt" who was once so renowned a knight (1750). The lady not only restores Ywayn's reason and ability to speak, but also provides apparel, equipment, and a good palfrey to restore Ywayn's status (1759–1774).

34. Eugene Vance, *From Topic to Tale: Logic and Narrativity in The Middle Ages* Theory and History of Literature, Vol. 47 (Minneapolis: University of Minnesota Press, 1987), 54. Chapter 5, *"Si Est Homo, Est Animal,"* examines the story of Yvain and the hermit as an allegory of the origin of commerce.

35. Ibid., 70.

36. Unlike the beastly giant, Ywayn learns empathy for beasts from his life among the animals of the forest. In contrast with the giant who uses fear to control lesser beasts, the noble Ywayn forges a loyal bond with the regal lion that mimics the bond of fealty. By saving the lion from a dragon, traditionally another of Cain's kin, Ywayn earns the beast's

allegiance; from then on, the two travel and fight together as trusted companions. In an unusual reversal of the trope, the lion develops human attributes from his loyal service to the knight. When the lion later sees Ywayn bleeding, the beast roars in sorrow. Thinking Ywayn dead, the lion plans to slay himself by setting Ywayn's sword against a stone and running himself through (2071–84). When the lion is locked up by the two champions who fight Ywayn, he exhibits the response of a loyal retainer and reasons his way out of the locked chamber:

> Ful greet sorwe the leoun has
> In the chambre wher he was;
> And evere he thoughte upon that dede,
> How he was helped in his nede,
> And he myghte now do no socour
> To him that helped him in that stour:
> Myghte he out of the chambre breke,
> Soon he wolde his maister wreke,
> He herde her strokes that were ful sterne,
> And yerne waiteth in ilke heryne—
> And al was made ful faste to holde.
> Atte laste he cam to the thressh-holde:
> The erthe ther caste he up ful soon,
> As faste as four men sholde have don
> If they hadde broght bothe bille and spade;
> A muchel hole ful soon he made. (3211–26)

37. Chaucer, *The Knight's Tale,* 1656–58.

38. Ibid., 1721; 1740.

39. *Piers Plowman* B.II.164–77.

40. Ibid., Prol.146–49.

41. Ibid., Prol.150–51.

42. Ibid., Prol.148.

43. Ibid., Prol.156–57.

44. Hugh White, *Nature and Salvation in Piers Plowman* (Cambridge: Brewer, 1988), 19.

45. *Piers Plowman* B.XII.135–39.

46. Ibid., XII.107–112.

47. Ibid., XI.331–36.

48. Ibid., XI.369–72.

49. White, 19.

50. *Piers Plowman* B.V.270.

51. Ibid., XI.418–22.

52. Ibid., IV.30–33.

53. Ibid., IV.34–36.

54. Ibid., II.213–31.

55. Ibid., II.232–35.

56. Ibid., XX.349.

57. Ibid., XX.364.

58. Ibid., XX.378.

59. Ibid., IV.1–12.

60. Ibid., II.4.

61. Chaucer, *The Pardoner's Tale*, 760–75.

62. *Piers Plowman* B.II.24–28.

63. Ibid., II.119.

64. Ibid., XVI.8–9.

65. Ibid., XV.33.

66. 1 Cor 3:6–13.

67. Ibid., 3:15.

68. *Piers Plowman* B.Prol.64.

69. Simpson, 88.

70. Ibid., 89–92.

71. Ibid., 99.

72. *Piers Plowman* B.I.54–57.

73. Ibid., I.19.

74. Ibid., I.12–26.

75. Ibid., I.44–45.

76. Ibid., I.46–54.

77. Ibid., I.63–64.

78. Ibid., I.69–70.

79. Ibid., I.83–85.

80. Ibid., I.161–78.

81. Ibid., I.160.

82. Ibid., III.312.

83. See pp. 58–59 above.

84. *Piers Plowman* B.III.299–300.

85. Ibid., IX.202–3.

86. Ibid., IX.97.

87. Ibid., VIII.86; IX.98.

88. Ibid., VIII.91–92.

89. Ibid., VIII.96–99.

90. Ibid., IX.205–6.

91. Ibid., IX.100.

92. Ibid., XI.418–19.

93. Ibid., XII.107–11.

94. R. B. Dobson, *The Peasants' Revolt of 1381*, 2nd ed. (London and Basingstoke: The Macmillan Press LTD, 1983), 182.

95. Ibid., 185.

96. Ibid., 138.

97. Ibid., 173. Dobson 168–81 translates Walsingham, *Historia Anglicana*, I. 456–67.

98. Hilton notes that the rebels were not a homogeneous group, but practiced various occupations: "[O]n the basis of the indictments . . . there is a fair scattering—perhaps almost a substantial minority—of persons with other than agricultural occupations. Apart from the clergy . . . these are men who for the most part ply essential trades in any peasant society. Carpenters, sawyers, masons, cobblers, tailors, weavers, fullers, glovers, hosiers, skinners, bakers, butchers, innkeepers, cooks and a lime-burner are found in the Kentish indictments" (179). See also Christopher Dyer, "The Social and Economic Background to the Rural Revolt of 1381," in *The English Rising of 1381*, ed. R. H. Hilton and T. H. Aston (Cambridge: Cambridge University Press, 1984), who notes that while the rebels were generally "well below the ranks of the gentry," many of them were peasants and artisans who owned land and goods (15).

99. In *Hochon's Arrow: The Social Imagination of Fourteenth-Century Texts* (Princeton: Princeton University Press, 1992), Paul Strohm argues that the chroniclers employed such

strategies "to discredit the social standing, judgment, and objectives of the rebels at every level of representation" (34).

CHAPTER FIVE

1. Anne Hudson, "Piers Plowman and the Peasants' Revolt: A Problem Revisited," *The Yearbook of Langland Studies* 8 (1995), 86.

2. Cohn, 22–29.

3. For a detailed discussion of the challenges that these demographic shifts posed in the fourteenth century, see chapter 3 of this study.

4. Cohn, 31.

5. Ibid., 318.

6. Ibid.

7. Hilton, 179 discusses the varied composition of the rebel groups.

8. Ibid., 74.

9. Rossell Hope Robbins, "Middle English Poems of Protest," *Anglia* 78.2 (1960), 197.

10. Green, 192.

11. See Dobson 270–77; Walsingham, *Historia Anglicana*, I.467–73; II.27. Walsingham II.1–4 reports that the rebels of Bury St. Edmunds make a similar request, demanding that the monks "return the bonds by which the burgesses were bound to the king and the monastery" and "return the charters of liberties of the town which Cnut, the founder of the monastery, had once granted, and which his successors as kings to the present day had conceded for the security of the abbey" (Dobson 246).

12. Caroline M. Barron, "William Langland: A London Poet," in *Chaucer's England: Literature in Historical Context*, ed. Barbara Hanawalt (Minneapolis: University of Minnesota Press, 1992), 95.

13. Ibid.

14. Dobson, 127.

15. Strohm, 6. Cf., *The Sublime Object of Ideology* (London and New York: Verso, 1989), in which Slavoj Žižek explains that this "fundamental level of ideology" is "not of an illusion masking the real state of things but that of an (unconscious) fantasy structuring our social reality itself" (33).

16. Strohm, 34.

17. Chronicle reports that suggest the rebels planned to kill all clergy and nobles and to distribute the wealth of the kingdom resonate with panic and scorn and represent an official interpretation of the rebels' actions more than actual rebel goals.

18. Rossell Hope Robbins, *Historical Poems of the XIVth and XVth Centuries*. (New York: Columbia University Press, 1959), 59. Robbins entitles this 11-stanza poem from MS. Vernon f.411r, sometimes known by its refrain, "A *Warnyng to Be Ware*," as "The Insurrection and Earthquake." Walsingham also consistently depicts the rebellion as a form of divine retribution visiting England "as a chastisement for its sins" (Dobson, 132; see *Historia Anglicana*, I.453).

19. Dobson, 172.

20. Ibid.

21. Ibid., 172–75. As Sudbury fell, Walsingham reports he called out "Ah! Ah! this is the hand of God" (Dobson, 174; for Walsingham's account of the rebels in London, see *Historia Anglicana*, I. 456–67).

22. Ibid., 173. Dobson 168–81 translates Walsingham, *Historia Anglicana* I.456–67.

23. Ibid., 174–75.

24. *Knighton's Chronicle 1337–1396,* ed. and trans. by G. H. Martin. Oxford Medieval Texts. (Oxford: Clarendon Press, 1995), 215.

25. *Piers Plowman* B.XX.53–57.

26. Knighton, Walsingham and the "monk of Westminster" who recounts the events of the uprising in Higden's *Polychronicon*, IX.1–6 all report that the rebels labelled Sudbury and other targets as traitors.

27. Dobson, 201. Citing the Westminster chronicler's description of the heads' configuration, with Sudbury's "in the middle and above the others," Steven Justice describes how the display reflects the iconography of the Crucifixion: "Christ hangs between the two thieves and is foregrounded, so that his cross stands higher than the others; on his head, often red with blood, is the crown of thorns—meant as a mockery but actually a proclamation of the true kingship displayed in his suffering" (99).

28. Justice, 99.

29. While Cohn sees the rebels' use of "the time is now" as an indication that they expected the dawn of the Millennium or of "an egalitarian State of Nature" (215–17), the term could more simply reflect the language of the apocalyptic model as the predominant Christian model for social change. For late medieval Christians, the ideal model for Christian society was not prelapsarian, but feudal, their nostalgia not for an idealized classical past, but for an ideal feudal society.

30. See pp. 104–105, 108–109 below for more on the phrase "the time is now."

31. Walsingham, *Historia Anglicana* II.33–34; *Historia Angliae*, 322.

32. *Knighton's Chronicle 1337–1396*, 222.

33. Justice, 136.

34. Walsingham, Thomas. *Gesta abbatum monasterii Sacti Albani*. Ed Henry Thomas Riley. Rolls Series 28 London, 1869, 3:309. Justice translates: "[T]hey broke the stones into small pieces, giving some to each, just as it is customarily done in parish churches on Sunday to break and distribute the blessed bread, so that, when they saw these pieces, they would see for themselves that they had been victorious in their case against the monastery" (158).

35. For discussions of the millstone eucharist as a community sharing of the means of production, see Justice, 169; cf., Anne Middleton, "William Langland's 'Kynde Name': Authorial Signature and Social Identity in Late Fourteenth-Century England" in Lee Patterson, ed., *Literary Practice and Social Change in Britain, 1381–1530. (*Berkeley and Los Angeles: University of California Press, 1990), 72.

36. Justice, 159.

37. Ibid., 164–67.

38. *Knighton's Chronicle 1337–1396*, 222.

39. Ibid.

40. Justice, 186.

41. For a discussion on the authorship of the rebel messages, see pages 109–111 below.

42. Justice, 14–15, transcribed from BL Royal MS 13E.ix, fol. 287a; Walsingham *Chronicon Angliae*, 322.

43. *Knighton's Chronicle 1337–1396*, 222; 224.

44. Ibid.

45. Ibid., 224.

46. Justice, 138.

47. Carleton Brown and Rossell Hope Robbins, *The Index of Middle English Verse. (*New York: Columbia University Press, 1943), no. 2356.

48. Rossell Hope Robbins, ed., *Historical Poems of the XIVth and XVth Centuries*, xlii.

49. Rossell Hope Robbins, "Middle English Poems of Protest," 201.

50. Dobson, 379–80.

51. Hilton, 214.

52. Green, 182.

53. Justice, 20–21.

54. Ibid., 15

55. Ibid., 19, translating the *The Anonimalle Chronicle, 1333 to 1381*, ed. V. H. Galbraith. (Manchester, 1927), 135.

56. Green, 187.

57. Ibid.

58. Green, 189.

59. Kane, 90–91.

60. Green, 178.

61. See, for example, Maureen Quilligan's discussion of the various shades of meaning of the "trielich ymaked" tower at the beginning of *Piers Plowman* in *The Language of Allegory* (Ithaca and London: Cornell University Press, 1979), 58–62.

62. *Piers Plowman* B.XX.74–79.

CONCLUSION

1. *Pierce [Peres] the Ploughmans Crede*, ed. Walter W. Skeat. EETS. (London: Trübner & Co., 1867), 459.

2. Ibid., 464–57.

3. Ibid., 136.

4. Ibid., 397.

5. The Franciscan of *Peres the Ploughmans Crede* calls the wanderer "felawe" (102) in the hopes of gaining a contribution or securing the wanderer's loyalty to his order. Cf., the Dominican (243; 250). The Austin friar calls the wanderer "sone" in an attempt to woo him into support (306). The Carmelites also address the protagonist with flattery and unctious language, calling him "lef man" (372) and "leue leel man" (390).

6. *Peres the Ploughmans Crede*, 445–46.

7. Ibid., 473. When the plowman tells the wanderer his name, he replies, "A! Peres," a cry of recognition (474).

8. Ibid., 457.

9. Ibid., 458–61.

10. Ibid., 559.

11. Ibid., 603–8.

12. *Piers Plowman* B.VI.115–51.

13. *Peres the Ploughmans Crede*, 302–5.

14. Ibid., 330–32: "And þouȝ þou conne nouȝt þi Crede knele downe here; / My soule y sette for þyn to asoile þe clene, / In Couenaunt þat þou come againe & katell vs bringe."

15. Ibid., 336–37.

16. Ibid., 16–19.

17. Ibid., 20–23.

18. *Piers Plowman* B.VI.4.

19. Ibid., X.160–65.

20. *Peres the Ploughmans Crede*, 110–17.

21. Ibid., 123–29.

22. Ibid., 122.

23. Ibid., 175–80.

24. *Piers Plowman* B.XVI.86–89. Cf., *Piers Plowman* C.XVIII.122.

25. *Peres the Ploughmans Crede*, 189–90.

26. Ibid., 169–70.

27. Ibid., 216–18.

28. *Piers Plowman* B.III.40.

29. *Peres the Ploughmans Crede*, 752–55.

30. Ibid., 514.

31. Ibid., 515–18.

32. Ibid., 151.

33. See Chapter 5 above, pp. 104, 113-14.

34. *Peres the Ploughmans Crede*, 5–8.

35. *The Complaint of the Plowman*, ed. Thomas Wright. *Political Poems and Songs Relating to English History, Composed During the Period From the Accession of EDW. III. to that of RIC. III*, vol. 1 (London: Longman, Green, Longman, and Roberts, 1859), 304–46. Wright's edition does not include line numbers; the references to the poem that follow are cited by page number followed by stanza number in the published edition (with each page's stanzas numbered 1–4 except for the first and last pages, which contain only one stanza each).

36. *Piers Plowman* B.XX.354–79.

37. *The Complaint of the Ploughman*, 321 stanzas 1–3. The pelican wryly accuses the successor of Peter who mistreats his flock: "He culleth the sheepe as doth the cooke, / Of hem seeken the wool to rend, / And falsely glose the gospell booke."

38. Ibid., 341, stanzas 1–2.

39. Ibid., 329, stanza 3.

40. Ibid., 306, stanza 4.

41. Ibid., 325, stanza 2.

42. Ibid., 317, stanza 4.

43. Ibid., 336, stanza 4.

44. Ibid., 338, stanza 2. Cf., Eph. 6:13–18.

45. Ibid., 316, stanzas 2–3.

46. Ibid., 318, stanza 3.

47. Ibid., 343, stanza 4.

48. Ibid., 344, stanzas 3–4.

49. Ibid., 345, stanzas 1–2.

50. Ibid., 343, stanza 2.

51. The fist part of the poem had previously been referred to as *Richard the Redeless.*

52. *Mum and the Sothsegger*, ed. Mabel Day and Robert Steele. EETS. (London: Oxford University Press, 1936), Fragment M.48.

53. *Peres the Ploughmans Crede,* 486–502.

54. *Mum and the Sothsegger*, M.513–14.

55. Ibid., M.956–62.

56. Ibid., M.975–77.

57. Ibid., M.980–81.

58. Ibid., M.1293–1300.

59. Ibid., M.1726–33.

BIBLIOGRAPHY

Adams, John F. "Piers Plowman and the Three Ages of Man," *Journal of English and Germanic Philology* 61:1 (January 1962): 23–41.

Adams, Robert. "The Nature of Need in *Piers Plowman* XX," Traditio 34: 273–302.

Aers, David. *Chaucer, Langland and the Creative Imagination.* London: Routledge & Kegan Paul, 1980.

Alford, John A. *Piers Plowman: A Glossary of Legal Diction.* Cambridge: Brewer, 1988.

Ambrose, *De officiis ministrorum. Patrilogiae cursus completus, series Latina,* vol.XVI.

Andrew, Malcolm and Ronald Waldron, eds., *The Poems of the Pearl Manuscript.* Berkeley and Los Angeles: University of California Press, 1978.

The Anonimalle Chronicle. Edited by V. H. Galbraith. Manchester, 1927.

Augustine, *The City of God.*

_____ . *Commentary on the Lord's Sermon on the Mount with Seventeen Related Sermons.* Translated by Denis J. Kavanagh, O.S.A. New York: Fathers of the Church, Inc., 1951.

_____ . *Confessions.*

_____ . *On the Trinity.*

_____ . "Sermon 109," *Commentary on the Lord's Sermon on the Mount with Seventeen Related Sermons.* Translated by Denis J. Kavanagh. New York: The Fathers of the Church, 1951.

_____ . *Tractates on the Gospel of John.* Translated by John W. Rettig. The Fathers of the Church series, vol.78 Washington: The Catholic University of America Press, 1988.

Baker, Denise N. "From Plowing to Penitence: *Piers Plowman* and Fourteenth-Century Theology," *Speculum* 55:4 (October 1980): 715–25.

Baldwin, F. E. *Sumptuary Legislation and Personal Regulation in England.* Baltimore: The Johns Hopkins Press, 1926.

Barney, Stephen A. "The Plowshare of the Tongue: The Progress of a Symbol from the Bible to Piers Plowman," *Mediaeval Studies* 35 (1973): 261–93.

Barron, Caroline M., "William Langland: A London Poet." Chap. 5 in *Chaucer's England: Literature in Historical Context.* Edited by Barbara A. Hanawalt. Medieval Studies at Minnesota, vol. 4. Minneapolis: University of Minnesota Press, 1992.

Blake, N. F. *The Phoenix*. Manchester: Manchester University Press, 1964; reprint, Exeter: University of Exeter Press; Short Run Press, Ltd., 1990.

Bloomfield, Morton W. *Piers Plowman as a Fourteenth-Century Apocalypse*. New Brunswick, N.J.: Rutgers University Press, 1961.

Brown, Carleton and Rossell Hope Robbins. *The Index of Middle English Verse*. New York, 1943, no. 2356.

Brown, Peter. *Augustine of Hippo: A Biography*. Berkeley and Los Angeles: University of California Press, 1967.

Chambers, R. W. "Long Will, Dante, and the Righteous Heathen," *Essays & Studies* 9 (1924): 50–69.

Chaucer, Geoffrey. *The Works of Geoffrey Chaucer*. Edited by F. N. Robinson. Boston: Houghton Mifflin Company, 1957.

Clopper, Lawrence M. "Need Men and Women Labor?" Chapter 6 in *Chaucer's England: Literature in Historical Context.* Edited by Barbara A. Hanawalt. Medieval Studies at Minnesota, vol. 4. Minneapolis: University of Minnesota Press, 1992.

Coghill, Nevill K. "The Character of Piers Plowman Considered from the B Text," *Medium Ævum* 2:2 (June 1933): 54-86.

_____ . "The Pardon of Piers Plowman," *Proceedings of the British Academy* 30 (1946): 303-57; reprinted in Style and Symbolism in Piers Plowman: A Modern Critical Anthology. Edited by Robert L. Blanch. Knoxville: University of Tennessee Press, 1969, 40–86.

Cohn, Norman. *The Pursuit of the Millennium: Revolutionary Messianism in Medieval and Reformation Europe and Its Bearing on Modern Totalitarian Movements*, 2d ed., Harper Torchbooks, ed. Benjamin Nelson. New York: Harper & Row, 1961.

Dobson, R. B. *The Peasants' Revolt of 1381*, 2nd ed. London and Basingstoke: The Macmillan Press LTD, 1983.

Dunning, T. P. "Langland and the Salvation of the Heathen" *Medium Ævum* 12 (1943): 45–54.

Dyer, Christopher. "The Social and Economic Background to the Rural Revolt of 1381." Chap. in *The English Rising of 1381*. Edited by R. H. Hilton and T. H. Aston. Cambridge: Cambridge University Press, 1984.

Emmerson, Richard Keith. *Antichrist in the Middle Ages: A Study of Medieval Apocalypticism, Art, and Literature*. Seattle: University of Washington Press, 1981.

Emmerson, Richard K., and Ronald B. Herzman. *The Apocalyptic Imagination in Medieval Literature*. Philadephia: University of Pennsylvania Press, 1992.

Frank, Robert Worth, Jr. "The Pardon Scene in *Piers Plowman*," *Speculum* 26:2 (April 1951): 317–31.

Frantzen, Allen J. *The Literature of Penance in Anglo-Saxon England.* New Brunswick, NJ: Rutgers University Press, 1983.

Gimpel, Jean. *The Medieval Machine; The Industrial Revolution of the Middle Ages*, 2d ed. Cambridge: Wildwood House Limited, 1988.

Gower, John. Confessio Amantis. Edited by G. C. Macaulay. London: Oxford University Press, 1900.

Gradon, Pamela. "*Trajanus Redivivus*: Another Look at Trajan in *Piers Plowman*," in *Middle English Studies Presented to Norman Davis in Honour of His Seventieth Birthday.* Edited by Douglas Gray and E. G. Stanley. Oxford: Clarendon Press, 1983, 93–114.

Green, Richard Firth, "John Ball's Letters: Literary History and Historical Literature," Chapter 9 in *Chaucer's England: Literature in Historical Context*. Edited by Barbara A. Hanawalt. Medieval Studies at Minnesota, vol. 4. Minneapolis: University of Minnesota Press, 1992.

Hanawalt, Barbara A., ed. *Chaucer's England: Literature in Historical Context.* Medieval Studies at Minnesota, vol. 4. Minneapolis: University of Minnesota Press, 1992.

Hilton, Rodney. *Bond Men Made Free: Medieval Peasant Movements and the English Rising of 1381*. London: Routledge, 1973.

The Holy Bible, Douay-Rheims Version, revised by Bishop Richard Challoner, 1749–1752. Baltimore: John Murphy Company, 1899; reprint, Rockford, Illinois: TAN Books and Publishers, 1971.

The Jerusalem Bible, Reader's Edition. Garden City, NY: Doubleday & Company, 1966.

Kane, George, "Some Fourteenth-Century 'Political' Poems," in *Medieval English Religious and Ethical Literature: Essays in Honour of G. H. Russell.* Edited by Gregory Kratzmann and James Simpson. Cambridge, England: D.S. Brewer, 1986.

Kaske, R. E. with Arthur Groos and Michael W. Twomey. *Medieval Christian Literary Imagery: A Guide to Interpretation.* Toronto: University of Toronto Press, 1988.

Kerby-Fulton, Kathryn. *Reformist Apocalypticism and "Piers Plowman,"* Cambridge Studies in Medieval Literature, no. 7. Cambridge: Cambridge University Press, 1990.

Kermode, Frank. *The Sense of an Ending: Studies in the Theory of Fiction.* New York: Oxford University Press, 1967.

Knighton's Chronicle 1337–1396. Edited and translated by G. H. Martin. Oxford Medieval Texts. Oxford: Clarendon Press, 1995.

Langland, William. *Piers Plowman: the B Version. Will's Visions of Piers Plowman, Do-Well, Do-Better and Do-Best.* Edited by George Kane and E. Talbot Donaldson. London: University of London, Athlone Press, 1975.

———. *Piers Plowman by William Langland. An Edition of the C-text.* Edited by Derek Pearsall. York Medieval Texts, 2d series. London: Edsin Arnold Publishers, 1978.

Lawlor, John. "*Piers Plowman*: The Pardon Reconsidered," *Modern Language Review* 45:4 (October 1950): 449–58.

Le Goff, Jacques. *The Medieval Imagination.* Translated by Arthur Goldhammer. Chicago: The University of Chicago Press, 1988.

———. *Your Money of Your Life: Economy and Religion in the Middle Ages*, Translated by Patricia Ranum. New York: Zone Books, 1988.

Little, Lester K. *Religious Poverty and the Profit Economy in Medieval Europe*. Ithaca: Cornell University Press, 1978.

Mann, Jill. "Satisfaction and Payment in Middle English Literature," *Studies in the Age of Chaucer* 5 (1983): 17–47.

Mayhew, N. J. "Numismatic Evidence and Falling Prices in the Fourteenth Century." *The Economic History Review*, series 2, 27.1 (1974): 1–15.

McLeod, Susan H. "The Tearing of the Pardon in Piers Plowman," *Philological Quarterly* 56:1 (Winter 1977): 14–26.

Middle English Dictionary. Edited by Hans Kurath. Ann Arbor: University of Michigan Press, 1956.

Middleton, Anne, "William Langland's 'Kynde Name': Authorial Signature and Social Identity in Later Fourteenth-Century England" in *Literary Practice and Social Change In Britian, 1381–1530.* Edited by Lee Patterson. Berkeley and Los Angeles: 1990.

Miskimin, Harry A. *Cash, Credit and Crisis in Europe, 1300–1600.* London: Varorium Reprints, 1989.

____ . *The Economy of Early Renaissance Europe 1300-1460.* Englewood Cliffs, N.J.: Prentice-Hall, Inc., 1969.

____ . "The Enforcement of Gresham's Law," in *Credito, banche e investimenti, secoli XIII-XX: Atti della quarta Settimana di studio, Prato,* 14-21 April 1972, *Instituo Internazionale di Storia Economica 'F.Datini.* Florence: Felice le Monnier, 1985 reprint in *Cash, Credit and Crisis in Europe, 1300-1600*: 147-161.

____ . "Monetary Movements and Market Structure: Forces for Contraction in Fourteenth- and Fifteenth-Century England," *The Journal of Economic History* 24 (1964); reprint in Miskimin, *Cash, Credit and Crisis in Europe, 1300–1600*: 470–490.

____ . "Money and Money Movements in France and England at the End of the Middle Ages" in *Precious Metals in the Later Medieval and Early Modern Worlds.* Edited by J. F. Richards. Durham: Carolina Academic Press, 1983; reprint in Miskimin, *Cash, Credit and Crisis in Europe, 1300–1600:* 79–96.

Miskimin, Harry, R. S. Lopez, and A. Udovitch. "England to Egypt, 1350-1500: Long-term Trends and Long-distance Trade," *Studies in the Economic History of the Middle East.* Edited by M.A. Cook, Oxford: Oxford University Press, 1970; reprint in *Cash, Credit and Crisis in Europe, 1300-1600*: 93–128 .

Mum and the Soothsegger. Edited by Mabel Day and Robert Steele. Early English Text Society, original series, no. 199. London: Humphrey Milford, Oxford University Press, 1936.

Nightingale, Pamela. “Capitalists, Crafts and Constitutional Change in Late Fourteenth-Century London.” *Past & Present* 124 (August 1989): 3-35.

Orléan, André. “The Origin of Money” in *Understanding Origins*. Edited by Francisco J. Varela and Jean-Pierre Dupuy. Translated by Paisley Livingston. The Netherlands: Kluwer Academic Publishers, 1992, 113–143.

Ormrod, W. M. “The Peasants’ Revolt and the Government of England.” *Journal of British Studies* 29.1 (January 1990): 1–30.

_____ . *The Reign of Edward III: Crown and Political Society in England 1327–1377*. New Haven: Yale University Press, 1990.

Owst, G. R. “The ‘Angel’ and the ‘Goliardeys’ of Langland’s Prologue,” *Modern Language Review* 20:3 (July 1925): 270–9.

Patrides, C.A. *The Phoenix and the Ladder: The Rise and Decline of the Christian View of History*. Berkeley: University of California Press, 1964.

Pierce the Ploughmans Crede. Edited by Walter W. Skeat. EETS. London: Trübner & Co., 1867.

Plato, *Timaeus*.

Postan, M.M. *Essays on Mediaval Agriculture and General Problems of the Medieval Economy*. Cambridge: Cambridge University Press, 1973.

Prestwich, Michael. “Early Fourteenth-Century Exchange Rates.” *The Economic History Review* series 2, 32.4 (November 1979): 470–482.

Quilligan, Maureen. *The Language of Allegory*. Ithaca and London: Cornell University Press, 1979.

Reeves, Marjorie. *The Figurae of Joachim of Fiore*. Oxford: Clarendon Press, 1972.

_____ . *The Influence of Prophecy in the Later Middle Ages: A Study in Joachimism*. Oxford: Clarendon Press, 1969.

_____ . *Joachim of Fiore and the Prophetic Future*. London: SPCK, 1976.

Robbins, Helen, “A Comparison of the Effects of the Black Death on the Economic Organization of France and England,” *Journal of Political Economy*, 36 (1928): 447–79.

Robbins, Rossell Hope, ed., *Historical Piems of the XIVth and XVth Centuries*. New York: Columbia University Press, 1959.

———. "Middle English Piems of Protest," *Anglia,* 78.2 (1960): 193–203.

Ruding, R. *Annals of the Coinage of Great Britain and its Dependencies*, 1840.

Russell, J. C. *British Medieval Population.* Albuquerque: University of New Mexico Press, 1948.

Schroeder, Mary C. "*Piers Plowman*: The Tearing of the Pardon," *Philological Quarterly* 49:1 (January 1970): 8–18.

Simpson, James. "Spirituality and Economics in Passus 1-7 of the B Text," *Yearbook of Langland Studies* 1 (1987):83–103.

Skeat, Walter W., ed. *Pierce the Ploughmans Crede*. London: Early English Text Society, N. Trubner & Co., 1867.

———. Introduction to *The Vision of William Concerning Piers the Plowman, In Three Parallel Texts, Together with Richard the Redeless, By William Langland.* London: Oxford University Press, 1886; reprinted 1924, Vol. II.

Spearing, A. C. *Medieval Dream-Poetry*. Cambridge: Cambridge University Press, 1976.

Stevick, Robert D., ed. *Five Middle English Narratives*. Indianapolis and New York: Bobbs-Merrill Company, 1967.

Strohm, Paul. *Hochon's Arrow: The Social Imagination of Fourteenth-Century Texts.* Princeton: Princeton University Press, 1992.

The Transition from Feudalism to Capitalism, Verso edition. With an Introduction by Rodney Hilton. Norfolk, England: Thetford Press Limited, 1976.

Vance, Eugene. *From Topic to Tale: Logic and Narrativity in The Middle Ages.* Theory and History of Literature, Vol. 47. Minneapolis: Univeristy of Minnesota Press, 1987.

Wallace, David. "Chaucer and the Absent City." Chap in *Chaucer's England: Literature in Historical Context*, ed. Barbara Hanawalt. Medieval Studies at Minnesota, vol. 4. Minneapolis: University of Minnesota Press, 1992.

Walsingham, Thomas. *Chronicon Angliae*. Edited by Edward Maunde Thompson. Rolls Series 64. London, 1874.

Wells, Henry W. "The Construction of *Piers Plowman*," *PMLA* 44:1 (March 1929): 123-49.

Wetherbee, Winthrop. *Platonism and Poetry in the Twelfth Century: The Literary Influence of the School of Chartres*. Princeton: Princeton University Press, 1972.

Whatley, Gordon. "The Uses of Hagiography: the Legend of Pope Gregory and the Emperor Trajan in the Middle Ages," *Viator* 15 (1984): 25-63.

White, Hugh. *Nature and Salvation in Piers Plowman.* Cambridge: Brewer, 1988.

Williams, Raymond. *Keywords: A Vocabulary of Culture and Society*. New York: Oxford University Press, 1983.

Woolf, Rosemary. "The Tearing of the Pardon" in *Piers Plowman: Critical Approaches.* Edited by S. S. Hussey. London: Methuen, 1969, 50-75; reprinted in Woolf *Art and Doctrine: Essays on Medieval Literature.* London: The Hambledon Press, 1986, 131–56.

Wright, Thomas, ed. *Political Poems and Songs Relating to English History, Composed During the Period from the Accession of Edw. III to that of Ric. III*, vol 1. London: Longman, Green, Longman, and Roberts, 1859.

Wynnere and Wastoure. Edited by Sir Israel Gollancz. Oxford: Oxford University Press, 1921; reprint, Cambridge: D.S. Brewer Ltd., 1974.

Yunck, John A. *The Lineage of Lady Meed: The Development of Mediaeval Venality Satire*, Publications in Mediaeval Studies, ed. Philip S. Moore, C.S.C., no. 17. Notre Dame: University of Notre Dame Press, 1963.

Index

Adams, Robert, 50–51, 53, 143n, 144n
agricultural crisis, 6, 7, 58-61
agricultural imagery, 7, 12, 40–41, 43, 49, 51, 59, 74, 86-87, 102–103, 107, 126, 133n, 136n, 150n
Alain de Lille, 14, 24, 138n
Alford, John A., 149n
Ambrose, 51, 143n
Anonimalle Chronicle, 98, 110, 158n
Antichrist, 2, 6, 35, 48, 51–53, 75–76, 86, 99–102, 113–114, 120, 122, 124–125, 132n
Antichrist friar, 35, 52, 76, 85, 92, 116
Apocalypse. *See* Revelation, Book of
apocalypticism, 2, 3, 5, 11, 13, 13, 15–22, 25–28, 96–97, 99–102, 105–108, 113–114, 127; eschatology, 5, 11–17, 19, 26–28, 30, 53, 96–97; Final Days and The Second Coming, 15, 16, 19, 35, 132n; Judgment Day, 5, 14, 17–22, 28, 30, 49, 73, 85–86, 92, 136n; sheep and goats, 21, 76, 85. *See also* Millennium; New Jerusalem; *Piers Plowman* and apocalypticism; regeneration
apocalyptic urgency, 19, 34, 105, 108
Aquinas, Thomas, 51, 141n, 143n
Aristotle, 134n, 141n
Augustine of Hippo, 5, 12, 20–23, 26, 53, 134n, 135n, 141n, 150n; The City of God, 21–23
avarice, 1, 59, 83, 143n
Ball, John and his letters, 9, 13, 95–96, 101–102, 105–112, 126
Barney, Stephen A., 49, 143n
Barron, Caroline M., 97–98
Beowulf, 142n
Black Death, 1, 2, 8, 16, 26, 34, 56–58, 60–61, 65, 69–70, 96, 144n, 145n, 146n
Blake, N. F., 14
Bloomfield, Morton W., 12–13, 29, 49–50, 136n
Boethius, 23–24, 77–78, 135n. *See also* Chaucer: *Boece*
Cain, 46, 48–49, 80, 89, 115, 125, 151n
Carruthers, Mary S., 40
Chaucer, Geoffrey, 75; *Boece*, 24, 77; *The Canterbury Tales*: 34, 62, 73; 75–76, 80, 85, 135n, 149n; *Parlement of Foules*, 77, 135n
Cleanness, 79
Clopper, Lawrence M., 31
clothing and cloth, 9, 35, 50–51, 62–65, 68, 73, 88, 115–116, 123, 144n, 145n, 146n. *See also* wool market
Cohn, Norman, 3, 16, 18, 20, 22, 24–25, 96–97, 129n, 156n
coin and bullion shortages. *See* money
common good, 59, 71, 91
Complaint of the Plowman, 9, 122–124, 159n
concentration of wealth, 50, 60
consumption patterns, 56

conspicuous consumption, 50, 52, 62–64, 67–68
Corpus Christi, Feast of, 103–104
Crusades, 18, 22
Daniel, Book of, 16, 78, 80, 131n, 150n
degeneration, man to beast, 78–81, 83, 115 ;and rebels, 8, 93–94, 100, 150n, 151n
demographic shifts, 3, 78, 55–58, 68
Dieulacres Abbey Chronicle, 95
Dobson, R. B., 110
Domesday Survey, 56
dowel, *dobet*, and *dobest*, 5, 9, 13, 39–40, 53, 77, 91–92, 95–96, 105, 139n; and the 1381 revolt, 95-96, 105, 140n
Ecclesiastes, Book of, 17, 136n
economic development, 3, 55–65, 68–69
economic discourse, 7–8, 30, 35–36, 55, 71
Edward III, 66, 73
estates and *status*, 4–5, 12, 31–32, 39, 45, 49, 63, 72, 74, 77, 81, 93. *See also* feudalism
Exeter Book, 14
famine, 2, 16, 52–53, 56–57, 96, 132n, 145n. *See also* hunger
fellowship and *felawes*, 71–73, 75–80, 83–86, 89–90, 102, 105–106, 108, 113, 116, 119, 149n, 158n
feudalism, 12, 47, 58, 68–69, 71, 91–93, 96, 126–127, 151n
Final Days. *See* apocalypticism
food: bread, 76, 103-104; production, 58, 88, 105; spending on, 61. *See also* famine
Francis of Assissi, 36, 41, 76, 118–119
Frantzen, Allen J., 138n
friars, 34–36, 41, 116–121, 125, 138n , 158n. *See also* Antichrist friar
Froissart, 93
gift economy, 1, 47
Gollancz, Sir Israel, 73
Gower, John, 59, 93, 99
Green, Richard Firth, 97, 110, 112–113
Hawkin, 50, 56, 89, 92
Henry IV, 126
Hilton, Rodney, 3–4, 6, 69, 110, 130n, 154n
Hobbe the robber, 95, 104, 107, 111
Holy Church, 1–2, 6, 30, 35, 46–47, 75–76, 85–89, 92, 116, 120
Hudson, Anne, 95
hunger, 22, 38–40, 51–52, 56–57, 88, 125. *See also* famine
Irenaeus, 20, 133n
Joachim of Fiore, 24–25
justice and injustice, 2, 5–8, 11, 29–31, 33, 38, 40, 43, 45–46, 50, 52, 69–70, 75–76, 84, 90–91, 96–98, 102–103, 106–107, 113, 123, 127, 136n
Justice, Stephen, 101–106, 108–110, 156n, 157n
just price, 45–46
Kane, George, 112
Kaske, R. E., 21, 133n
Kerby-Fulton, Kathryn, 13, 24, 53
kings and kingship, 31, 48, 52–53, 74–75, 84, 91–92, 98
Knighton, Henry, 93, 100–102, 104–105, 107–108
Kynde, 77, 81–84, 90, 94
Kynde Wit, 81–84, 87, 90–91
labor. *See* work
labor shortages, 57, 68
Lactantius, 14, 20
Langland, William, 2, 4–5, 8–9, 13, 19, 29, 31–36, 38–40, 43, 45–53, 55, 57–60, 70–77, 81–85, 87–100, 105–106, 113, 115, 117–118, 120–122, 126–127, 141n
Le Goff, Jacques, 30, 37, 45, 137n, 138n, 141, 143n
Little, Lester, 1, 35, 37, 47, 138n, 141n
locus amoenus, 27, 126, 135n
Lucifer, Satan, 21, 48, 79, 90, 124
luxury and luxury goods, 60–65, 68–70, 148n

Mann, Jill, 144n
market economy, 3–4, 36, 39, 45, 47, 55–70
Mayhew, N. J., 56, 65
measure, moderation, 50–51, 88, 94
Meed, 1–2, 8, 19, 50–51, 70, 74, 78, 80, 84–85, 87–89, 91, 98, 142n
Meed's retinue, 8, 76, 80, 84–85
Millennium, millenarianism, 3, 5–6, 8, 11, 15–22, 25–27, 48, 96–97, 133n, 144n, 156n. *See also* apocalypticism
mining, 65
minting. *See* money
Miskimin, Harry A., 6, 55–61, 64, 66–67, 69, 144n, 145n, 146n, 147n
money, 140n, 141n; "good money,"65–67; peril of, 1–2, 47–48, 59; 142n; supply and bullion shortages, 7, 60, 63–66, 69, 148n; versus treasure, 47, 142n. *See also* treasure
moneylending, 36, 141n
monks and monasticism, 34, 103, 144n, 155n, 157n
Mum and the Sothsegger, 9, 125–127
need, 50–53, 143n, 144n
Neoplatonism, 14, 22–23
New Jerusalem, 5, 16–18, 21, 26–27
Nightingale, Pamela, 70
nostalgia, 12. *See also* radical nostalgia
occupations, 32–33, 36, 39; primary, seconday, and tertiary, 44–45, 140n
Ordinance of 1349, 69
Origen, 20, 23
Orléan, André, 47, 142n
Ormrod, W. M., 70
Owst, G. R., 110, 137n
Patrides, C. A., 14, 17
Pearl, 26–28
Peasant's Revolt. *See* Revolt of 1381
penance, 30, 35, 42; and economic metaphors, 30, 33, 36–37
perfection, 29–30, 50, 91–92, 105
phoenix, *The Phoenix*, 23, 124
Piers Plowman, 1–2, 5–6, 8–9, 11–13, 28–35, 37–43, 46–53, 55–59, 64, 70–78, 80–96, 98, 104–107, 109, 113–121, 124, 141n; and apocalypticism, 2, 5, 11–13, 49–53, 74, 86, 93, 95–96, 144n; belling the cat, 32, 80–81, 91; fruit of Piers, 49, 85–86; pardon incident, 38, 40–42; and rebel letters, 95. *See also dowel*, *dobet* and *dobest*; Hawkin; hunger; Langland; Meed; Will the dreamer
Pierce the Ploughman's Crede, 9, 115–123, 125
pilgrims and pilgrimage, 11–12, 14, 53, 135n
plague. *See* Black Death
Plato, 23, 131n. *See also* Neoplatonism
poll tax. *See* taxation
Postan, M. M., 7, 56
poverty and the poor, 34, 36, 42, 50, 63, 83; apostolic poverty, 41–42, 48, 76, 89, 118
pricing trends, 56, 58–60, 63, 145n
professions. *See* occupations
profit economy, 1, 29, 71
Quilligan, Maureen, 158n
radical nostalgia, 5, 12–13
Revolt of 1381, 2, 4, 68, 59, 68, 70, 72, 91, 95–114, 126–127
rebels and rebel leaders, 6–7, 9, 94–104, 107–114, 154n; rebel demands, 96–98, 103–106; rebel letters, addresses, 95–96, 101–108, 111–112; Jack Carter, 95, 101–102, 104–107, 111–112; Jack Milner, 101–108; Jack Trewman, 101–102, 105–108
redde quod debes, 29–31, 136n
redemption, 2, 86
Reeves, Marjorie, 25
renovation mundi, regeneration, 1–5, 11–15, 19–20, 22, 31, 53
restitution. *See* penance; satisfaction
Revelation, Book of, 16, 22, 24, 26, 125, 131n , 136n

Richard II, 67, 69, 98, 124
Robbins, Helen, 57
Robbins, Rossell Hope, 97, 109, 112
Russell, J. C., 56
sacrifice, 6, 21, 29, 43–45, 47
Saint Albans, 97, 103–104, 110, 157n
salvation, 2, 6, 9, 29–31, 40, 43, 49, 75, 86. *See also* redemption
satisfaction, 2, 6, 36–37, 46
Savoy, 104, 110
Simon Magus, simony, 33, 137n
Simpson, James, 29, 87, 142n
Skeat, Walter W., 9, 11
society. *See* fellowship
Spearing, A. C., 24
Statute of Laborers, 69
Strohm, Paul, 98–99, 154n
Sudbury, Simon, 97, 100–101, 156n
Sumptuary Act of 1363, 63
taxation, 4, 60, 66, 69, 88–89, 119
Third Age. *See* Millennium
trade imbalance, 63–64
treasure, earthly versus heavenly, 13, 32, 35, 38, 44, 46–47, 87, 89, 117–120
Treasury of Merits, 36
trewemen, 13, 19, 101. *See also* rebels
Truth, 46–47, 75, 84, 87–89, 92, 97, 106, 109, 112
Unity. *See* Holy Church
Vance, Eugene, 79–80
venality satire, 1, 55
Wallace, David, 149n
Walsingham, Thomas, 94, 99–100, 102–108, 110, 146n, 155n, 156n, 157n
wastours, 32, 40, 56, 74, 92, 117, 126; *See also Wynnere and Wastoure*
Westminster Chronicle, 101, 156n
Wetherbee, Winthrop, 23, 134n
White, Hugh, 81, 83
Will the dreamer, 12, 35, 37–38, 52–53, 57, 71, 83, 88, 92, 116, 121
Williams, Raymond, 12, 72
wool market, 7, 59, 64, 145n. *See also* cloth
work, and salvation, 6, 9, 28, 37–39, 40, 42–43, 45, 49. *See also* occupations
Wyclif, John and Wycliffites, 115, 121–122, 125
Wynnere and Wastoure, 73–74
xenophobia, 3, 70
Yunck, John A., 1, 55
Yvain, ou le chavalier au lion, 79
Ywayn and Gawayne, 79–80, 151n

Studies in the Humanities

Edited by Guy Mermier

The Studies in the Humanities series welcomes manuscripts discussing various aspects of the humanities. The series' emphasis is on medieval and Renaissance literatures with a focus on Western civilizations and cultures. Submissions dealing with linguistics, history, politics, or sociology within the same time frame and geographical bounds are also encouraged. Manuscripts may be submitted in English, French, or Italian. The preferred style manual is the MLA Handbook (1995).

For additional information about this series or for the submission of manuscripts, please contact:

Peter Lang Publishing, Inc.
Acquisitions Department
516 N. Charles St., 2nd Floor
Baltimore, MD 21201